Let Us Learn Limba
Miŋ Thaniya Hulimba

John-Paul Conteh

Sierra Leonean Writers Series (SLWS)

Let Us Learn Limba
Miŋ Thaniya Hulimba

ISBN: 978-9988-8698-6-1

Sierra Leonean Writers Series
120 Kissy Road Freetown, Sierra Leone
Kofi Annan Avenue, North Legon, Accra, Ghana
Publisher: Prof. Osman Sankoh (Mallam O.)
publisher@sl-writers-series.org
www.sl-writers-series.org

Table of Contents

Acknowledgements

My sincere gratitude goes first and foremost to my Professors in the Department of Modern Languages at FBC, Mr Gabriel Turay and Dr Bai E Sharka, who took me African Languages in my undergraduate Linguistics Course. My gratitude also goes to the HoDs of Language Arts, Indegineous Languages, and Education at Northern Polytechnic for their invaluable contributions in proof-reading my manuscript and restructuring the chapters. My special thanks also go to the Principal and the Registrar of NP for allowing me to do my first presentation on campus and for actually participating in the subsequent discussions. I owe gratitude to the team of Limba language <u>experts,</u> led by Rev.P.A.Sesay, Inspector of Schools, Bombali District and Rev. Daniel M Mansaray an undergraduate student at Northern Polytechnic who made a critique of my manuscript and rendered valuable suggestions for improvement. I am also grateful to Mr Samuel Tamba, HoD of Language Arts, Eastern Polytechnic, Kenema Campus, who edited the typescript and made invaluable remarks.

John-Paul Conteh

Preface

This piece of work is a humble attempt at preparing a source book for the teaching of Limba language in schools and colleges. It has been observed by linguists that the Limba ethnic group has got the largest number of dialects in Sierra Leone. There are at least 12 dialectal variations in Limba but only five are most significant in that they have got a very large number of speakers. These are **Biriwa, Safroko, Sella, Tonko and Wara Wara**. The other dialects are a sub-set of either one or two of the bigger dialects. For example, **Bimankoh** is a subset of Biriwa and Safroko; **Bikelen** is a subset of Biriwa and Songo, and Kalanthuba; **Bisonko** is a subset of Kelen and Wara Wara; while **Kalanthuba** is a subset of Safroko, Simiria and Biriwa; the **Simiria** is a subset of Safroko and Kalanthuba, slightly influenced by Themne and Koranko. The **Kamukeh** dialect is a mixture of Wara Wara, Yalunka and Fula who surround them in Koinadugu district.

It is also observed that the small quantum of written materials in Limba is heavily influenced by Tonko and Sela Limba. School children of other dialects other than the two are often faced with a gross disadvantage when taking the Limba Language at Basic Education Certificate Examinations (BECE) to mark the completion of Junior Secondary School (JSS). The reason is that the few Tonko/Sela writers do not take cognizance of the dialectal variations at least among the five major groupings.

It is worthy to note also that although Limba is among the four examinable National Languages at BECE level, it was not taught in Northern Polytecnic until recently in 2010 when I presented this manuscript to the college authorities. It is still not taught in Port Loko Teachers College because the manuscript has not been presented to the college authorities. Besides, the college authorities claim to have difficulties in recruiting lecturers for Limba Language.

Ironically the Northern Region is the home of the Limba ethnic group. They are found in all five districts. The three major dialects - Biriwa, Safroko and Sella - are playing host to Northern Polytechnic in Bombali District. The Tonko Limba of TMS Chiefdom in Port

Loko District and those in Tonko Limba Chiefdom in Kambia District, play host to Port Loko Teachers College. Limba students in these Education Colleges are forced to study Themne Language, the only option. Because they are non-native speakers of Themne, especially the Biriwa, Wara Wara, Sonko, Kalanthuba and Sela, their results in the Final Year examinations in Northern Polytechnic, especially before the introduction of the Limba Language course, were often poor. Most Limba students merely receive a pass in Themne Language.

It is my desire that the Limba Language is taught in the two Teacher Training Colleges in the Northern Region, and in Junior Secondary Schools; hence my undertaking of this project. I have taken consideration of the dialectal variations and have come up with what I dub **Synonymy** in Limba. This will enable students to understand each other's dialect without difficulty and to appreciate each other better. It will also encourage Limba students and pupils to be proud of their language. Above all, this work could be a point of reference for non-Limba speakers who are interested in speaking the language.

The intended source book is merely a guide to the teaching of Limba in schools and colleges. It is not an encyclopaedia or a dictionary. Therefore do not expect to see all the words/expressions that exist in the Limba language. The source book is in fact subject to regular updating based on feed-back from readers of the book. You will notice that some aspects – expressions, idioms are repeated. This is consciously done for emphasis.

A Short History of the Limba

Historically the Limba are said to have been the only aborigines of Sierra Leone who had occupied the Wara Wara Mountains in Koinadugu District, Northern Sierra Leone. Over the centuries, they had migrated southwards and northwest occupying lands that are today called Bombali, Port Loko, Kambia and Tonkolili districts. Those who remained in the Wara Wara Mountain range in Koinadugu District are known as the Wara Wara, Sonko and Kamukeh. Those that settled in Bombali District are the Biriwa, Safroko and Sella. Kelen – a mixture of Biriwa and Sonko; and Bimanko - a mixture of Biriwa and Safroko, who also live in Bombali District, in the east and south of the district. The Sella Limba speakers are the group that occupied the north of Bombali, while the Tonko are those that crossed over the Little Scarcies River in Kambia District and TMS Chiefdom in Port Loko District in the North-West Region. Those that live in the north of Tonkolili are referred to as the Simiria and Kalanthuba. Both dialects have got a heavy mixture of Safroko and slightly Koranko.

The Limba ethnic group is the third largest in Sierra Leone after Mende and Themne.

Social life among the Limba people

The Limba people are traditionally farmers engaged in subsistence farming. Farming is done mainly on upland where intercropping is possible. Sorghum, pearl millet, sesame/benni, corn, konso, beans, broad beans are among the crops grown alongside the rice. Swampland cultivation is also done among the Limba. With the exception of Tonko Limba land, groundnut cultivation both on upland and swampland is generally seen as a woman's job. When the women harvest their groundnuts, cash accrued from sales of the crop is expected to augment the husband's expenditure on children's school fees, medicare and clothing. In a few households, however, women do everything for their children, and to clothe themselves.

In the olden days, a decade or two before independence, the Limba youths travelled to the capital city, Freetown, to do menial jobs for the Creole elite. Through this many youths had received western education from their employers, the Creoles. Many others took up employment as unskilled labourers in the sea port – at Sierra Leone Ports Authority (SLPA) and Sierra Leone Produce Marketing Board (SLPMB). A few other Limba youth who never received western education, took up petty trading (one-man business) and the trades – carpentry, masonry, plumbing, fitting etc.

The Limba are a very peaceful and law-abiding people. They are respectful and humble, sometimes even to a fault, especially the women. In colonial days their humility had earned them both respect and western education for a few. Because of their humility, they were often the favourites of the Creole people to serve them as house boys. Some Creole masters afforded to educate their house boys by sending them to school. They adopted the Limba boys as their children and gave them Creole family names. It is not surprising then that we hear of the P M Johnsons, the Pratts and J S Findleys of Tonko Limba, the H A Palmers of Bumban, Biriwa, the Joe Paul-Wrights of Safroko Limba, the Macmillan's of Sela Limba, to name but a few. In Biriwa Chiefdom, for example, the late H. A. Palmer (Rtd. Commissioner of Police) was a Conteh, an uncle of mine. He died in June 2007. Alie Conteh was adopted by a certain

Mr Palmer, a Creole, in Freetown. Mr Palmer gave his adopted son the Christian name Henry and the Creole family name, Palmer. As a result of the Creole family name, Henry Alie Palmer, like Patrick M Johnson and a few others, received rapid promotions in the Sierra Leone Police Force before he was retired in the late 1980s.

The Limba are a people who are willing to do odd jobs, even very hard tasks. Carrying heavy load and working under difficult conditions is the lot of the average traditional Limba man. Note that traditional here means the stark illiterate man who really upholds and respects his culture. In the good old days before the onset of the rebel war, when the Sierra Leone Ports Authority (SLPA) was booming with cargo ships and the Sierra Leone Produce Marketing Board (SLPMB) was in full operation, about 70% of the unskilled labour work force was Limba. This status quo started changing in the 1960s when more Limba children started gaining access to western education. The youth of today are very selective in doing hard jobs and are less humble.

Palm wine is the commonest beverage among the Limba. The skill of palm wine tapping is inherent among many Limba groups, especially those communities where we have a preponderance of wild palm trees as in Safroko Limba Chiefdom. It is in these communities also that we have the highest production of palm oil. Palm wine is very useful during the farming season as food drink, entertainments, marriages, funeral observances, mourning, death anniversaries, to name but a few. The fact that the Limba are the most talented in palm wine tapping does not mean that every Limba child drinks palm wine. In fact, there are a few palm wine tappers who have never tasted palm wine. Through palmwine tapping a few boys are said to have paid there their own school fees and school charges to attain secondary education.

Among all the ethnic groups of Sierra Leone, the Limba are considered to be the most skilled in palm wine-tapping. In Limba country, palm wine is not only used for entertainment purposes, it is also used as food for work. In some communities palm wine is offered to strengthen the bonds of marriage. When a suitor/husband visits his in-laws, he takes palm wine to offer them. Discussions are very lively where palm wine is served. When a youth wants to seek advice from an elderly man, he offers him palm wine. As food for work, male youth in a work group, for example, take some gallon/container of palm wine to share with members during lunch or break.

When the palm wine tappers arrived in a big settlement, they generally occupied the outskirts of the community – thus starting what people popularly call **Limba Corner**. As the natives extend their house construction scheme towards the palm wine-tapper's settlement, the Limba palm wine tappers move forewards to start yet another Limba Corner ; hence the big area that this Limba Corner spans in some big towns. Sometimes the Limba palm wine-tappers are no longer staying in these <u>Corners</u>. Yet the name remains. It is not surprising therefore to hear of Limba Corner in most big towns in the Themne and Mende regions. The truth is: the average Limba man is considerate, very peaceful, law abiding, avoids open confrontation with local authorities. As such they prefer starting their own settlements in the outskirts of the host town/village, removed from the watchful eye of local authorities who are most times Muslims and are generally opposed to palm wine drinking.

Moreover, the palm wine tappers get good patronage from youths whose parents are opposed to drinking when they settle in the corners. The youths can very easily sneak in to buy a cup/litre of palm wine. Some married women, whose husbands are opposed to drinking, also sneak in to drink palm wine in the Limba Corner – the economic factor. Above all, the Limba diaspora in the country comprises mainly palm wine tappers who earn their income from palm wine production. A few men go to mine diamond and gold or do petty trading.

Note that four groups/dialects – Safroko, Simiria, Kalanthuba and Songo - take the lead in the Limba diaspora propelled by palm wine-tapping. Go to Safroko, Simiria and Sonko chiefdoms, you can count a few zinc houses that were constructed by palm-wine tappers who had either returned home or built those houses for their relatives and went back to the <u>coast</u>. That is the big urban settlements or cities. During the months of February to May each year, most palm wine tappers return home to assist their relatives in the brushing and ploughing on upland-rice farms. Some go to support their relatives during initiation ceremonies (secret societies) or initiate their children. In some towns like Lunsar, Port Loko and Kambia for example, there is often a noticeable scarcity of palm wine during this period.

Music and Dance among the Limba

Like all Sierra Leonean tribes, the Limba use various types of musical instruments for various purposes, ranging from entertainment at work on the farms or play after harvest, funerals, anniversaries, secret societies or other ceremonies. There is music and dance before, during and after initiation into the secret societies. There is music and sometimes dance during brushing, ploughing, weeding and harvesting on the upland rice farms. There is music and dance to celebrate end-of-harvest on the rice farms. There is music and dance to placate/appease the ancestors or spirits before active farming starts or before taking any communal venture. There is music and dance to bury the dead or mourn with the bereaved. There is music and dance to celebrate death anniversaries, etc.

The common musical instruments used among the Limba include; the drum (hubaŋ), kusuŋ, husambori, dundu, huthamba (hand drum) nkali, bira, kɔnthɔbende/sɛnikɛlɛ, kontho, husaaka, kuthuthu, kututɛŋ, kuthodo,konkoma, huyenkerima,yakuyŋ, bubu, Kurɔki, kubilo, hankulu(angle) kankara, kɛnkɛŋn etc.

Season/ Occasion	Type of music/dance	Musical instruments
Carefree/after harvest	Pɔrɔ,bira, bondo, kuthodo,thegbe,mathɔŋ	Drum(hubaŋ), kelen, angle, kongoma, box,bira, hand drum(huthamba) etc
Brushing upland	Bira	Bira
Weeding	Bira,nkali (kelen)	Bira, nkali, kɔnthɔbende...
Harvesting	Bira, mathɔŋ,	Bira, nkali, drum, flute,etc
Men's initiation	Gbondokali, kugbɛkɛti, pɔrɔ, tiyɛ, kudɛgbɛlɛ, makoloŋ	Band/drum, shakers(yakuin), kelen, drum, ...
Women's initiation	Kukanthaŋ, bondo, mayɛnyɛ,	Sambori,bondo drum, shegureh
Funerals	Kuyogba(solemn match past of society women at the death of a member) tiyɛ (men's secret society dance), humɛndaŋ - a special dance - secret society for distinguished women	Sambori, segureh, kontho, kelen
Death anniversary	Huboka, kukanthi, masande, ma Gbendekɔlɔ, huwosi, kuthodo, dari (mayaari)	Dundu, baŋ, kelen, kusuŋ, kuthuthu, kɛnkɛŋ, etc
Accompanying a bride to her groom (by women)	gbongbo	1. Bondo drum,shakers etc.

CHAPTER 1

The Phonology of Limba

Section 1

1.   The Sound System
      Vowels, Consonants, Diphthongs, Prenasals
2.   Syllable formation
3.   Noun class system (10)

1.1 – The Sounds of Limba

The Limba language has 25 sounds as follows:

a b s d i ɛ f g h y k e l m n o p u w ɔ ŋ gb th r t

1.1.1.   - Vowel Sounds – ŋatoŋa ŋa pothi

There are 7 vowel sounds in Limba. See below:

e i a o u ɔ ɛ

1.1.2 – Consonant Sounds - ŋatoŋa
There are 18 Consonant Sounds as follows:
b s d f g h y k l m n p r t w gb th ŋ

Note: the sounds 'ch' **j, v, z** do not exist in Limba, except in
         borrowed words.

1.1.3 – Diphthongs - ŋatoŋa

ɔy, ɛy, uy, ay, ey, au
f) y – a rat; ap) y – to stop; akuy – to fast; adey – to----; na fau – to
     be grey

1.1.4 - Prenasals

mb, mp, nth, nk

Eg. Mbɔɔ - a knife; mpɛɛthɛ - potatoes; mpati - children; ntha - something; nthonaŋ – sickness, nkɔnti - neck

1.   The Sound System
        -       Vowels, Consonants, Diphthongs, prenasals sounds
                (to be accompanied by symbols/pictures).

2.   Syllable formation

3.   Noun class system (10)

Singular		**Plural**
	Suffixes	
Hu	tha	ni
Bu	ŋa	bi - (prefix plural)
'n	-ni	ma - (liquids, manner
of		
'm	-ŋ, ɛŋ	ba - (doer of "ba"
Wu		
ku		

hati (a child); mpati (children)
bi (belonging to)
Mu (diminutive plural prefix)

Infinitive prefix - ba)

ba yɔla - to farm/plough/strive
ba kama - to dance
ba thara - to run

ma - too many
Mayaba (onions); magbengbe (pepper); makoloŋ(seeds)
                        mpati

haŋ - for a while   ka

       mu – (where to)

wu   - belong to; also small   bi

       ma - (verb) where to

maŋ - a stand alone suffix to liguids; adverbs of manner

       ma

1.2 – Sounds in Context

A. Vowels

e   - as in **e**! Exclamation, surprise

i   - as in as in **yiki** - respect

a   - as in abɔy – plenty; as in **yaaka**- charity

o   - as in fo - foxas in **foo**- fox

u   - as in – bu - fire

ɔ   - as in abɔy (plenty); adɔy – to labour

ɛ   - as in thɛ – fowl/chikenas in **hɛ/fɛ**

       (today)

1.2.1 – Diphthong/Glides

ɔ y – as in f ɔy (a rat); **adɔy**   - to toil/labour

ɛ y – as in dey – to belch   -   as in **kubey**   - a kernel

uy - as in ----   -   as in **buy**   - fire; akuy   - to abstain

ay – as in fay - slaughter   -   as in **afay**   - to slaughter;

akay - to go;

athay - to dry in the sun

ey   -   as in key (went)

       au – as in ------ -   as in **fau**   - grey

ɔy – as in abɔy – plenty, as in fɔy **(a rat or dig yam)**

1.2.2 - Prenasals

     mb   - as in mbɔɔ (knife); mbompa (a leaf); mbapu (camel)

     mp   - as in mpati (children); mputu (patched rice)

     nth   - as in nthaa (something); nthonaŋ (an illness/disease)

     nk - as in nkɔnti (neck); nko/nkoyo (throat)

     mb - as in mbompa (a leaf) - as in mbaana (a banana leaf);mboma–an illness/disease

3

mp - as mpati (children) - as in mpa, mputu, mpɛthɛ, mpɔyaŋ

nth - ntha (something)- as in nthaani (some things); nthaka, nthonaŋ

nk - as in nko (throat) - as in nkothi (foot path); nkala (a rope); nkali (kelen)

nt - as in ntutɛŋ (intestine)

1.2.3 - Consonants

b - as in bɛti (bird); bahu (goat); bɛthɔ (girl); boli(gold) bɛki (bag)

s - as in sa (come); sisa(bring); sisaa (rice); sigba (daggar); sira (Sarah); sama (Sama)

d - as in deka (idol); doni(load); danka(hook), dama (to hunt); dɔ nthɔ.. debt-

f - as in fothi (mouth/tell a lie); fɛ (today); fefa (head); feli (bush); feeli(egg), fati (a child); fatha(strength)

g - as in **paga (rice); taga** (sheep) in Tonko especially)

h - as in hati (child): hintima (darkness); huntuma (darkness); hɛkiŋ (this year); hɛra (winnow/chance)

y - as in yiki (respect); yi (you); yɔ la (plough/strive); yala (net/hammock, Allah), yɛla, yimbeŋ, yáraba

k - as in **kaa (go); ka-(at); kappa (scratch), kɔ pa** (crack nut/stone); kumpa (spoon); kɔɔ sɛ (a horn);

l - as in lema (follow); lɔ sa(draw); laathu (a sling), lɔ nka (to lock); luka (tie); limaa (a sharping knife)

m - as in mɛti (town/village); mɛeti (salt); malo (joy/happy); mala (jump); malina (to light)

n - as in niya (make); nɛka (ook/observe); nɔ rɔ ,--ill luck); nɔ tha (shift); ninkire (a calf)

p - as in papa (papa/daddy); pɔ tha (squeeze), pitha (wear/put on); pila (cure); paya (sow/scatter); paaya (July)

r - as in rɔgba (hide); hu-ɽonko (ronko); huɽoŋa (tail of bird);

t - as in tali/tɛni (medicine); tala (lay); taka (sheep); tama (rub oil/greese); tɛpa (say/tell); tuma (take up lodging); tɔla (mend/tame)

w - as in wɔ/wa (someone);wɔ mɛti (a human being/ person), w ɔkita, wathe, ku-waatha, ba-wɛthi, ku-wera, wasa.wasi

4

gb - as in gbaku (chief); gboŋa(road); gbasa(mark); gbaya (cut); gbekedɛn (stilts); ku-gbeke (upper arm); hu-gbada (compound/homestead); gbaka (request/a big deer)

th - as in thɔma (eat); thunkuna(pay); thuŋunande (gather); thubuta(measure); thaya (dry in the sun); thaaya(eyes); thiita (include); thooti (nests); thaniya (learn)

ŋ - as in ŋaka, ŋaaka, ŋɔna, ŋuna adɔŋ, (ayɛnti) adiŋ, adɛŋ, adaŋ

1.3 – Syllable Formation

	e	i	a	o	u	ɔ	ɛ
b	be	bi	ba	bo	bu	bɔ	b ɛ
s	se	si	sa	so	su	sɔ	s ɛ
d	de	di	da	do	du	dɔ	d ɛ
f	fe	fi	fa	fo	fu	fɔ	f ɛ
g	ge	gi	ga	go	gu	gɔ	g ɛ
h	he	hi	ha	ho	hu	hɔ	h ɛ
y	ye	yi	ya	yo	yu	yɔ	y ɛ
k	ke	ki	ka	ko	ku	kɔ	k ɛ
l	le	li	la	lo	lu	lɔ	l ɛ
m	me	mi	ma	mo	mu	mɔ	m ɛ
n	ne	ni	na	no	nu	nɔ	n ɛ
p	pe	pi	pa	po	pu	pɔ	p ɛ
r	re	ri	ra	ro	ru	rɔ	r ɛ
t	Te	ti	ta	to	tu	t ɔ	t ɛ
w	We	wi	wa	wo	wu	wɔ	w ɛ
gb	Gbe	gbi	gba	gbo	gbu	gbɔ	gb ɛ
th	The	thi	tha	tho	thu	thɔ	th ɛ
ŋ	Ŋe	ŋi	ŋa	ŋo	ŋu	ŋu	ŋɛ

It is interesting to note that a few consonant sounds found in Krio/English are completely absent in Limba. These sounds are **ch, j, sh, v and g (tz,dz,s**...in English phonology) Except for the Tonko Limba, there is virtually no **g** sound in Limba. When the Limba is faced with pronouncing imported words (Krio, English) the light K sound is the close substitute. **Eg kot** for **goat, kem** for

game, kɔn for **gun, kren** for **grain** ---.The other sounds that are absolutely lacking in Limba are **v, sh, ch, j (dz)-**
When faced with pronouncing words with **v** in imported languages, the bilabial **b** or the **–w** are the close substitute eg **bot** for **vote, winto/binto** for **vimto, wɔmit/bɔmit** for vomit, **bɛst/wɛst** for vest

When faced with pronouncing words with **sh** in imported languages, the **s** is the close substitute
Sit for **sheet**
Sip for **sheep, Sɔt** for **short, sap** for **sharp, sek** for **shake**
sipi for **ship**

For imported words with **ch**, the close substitute is **t** eg
Tɔyt for **church, tita** for **teacher, prit** for **preach, blit** for **bleach,**

For imported words with **j (dz)** sound, the close substitute is **y** eg

Yɔn for **John, yomp** for **jomp, yɔmp** for **jump; yoke** for **joke, yɔt** for **jot, yun** for **June, yɛnuare** for **January, yɔyn** for **join, yisɔs** for **Jesus**

1.4 - Strong consonants in succession

It is important to note that very few words in Limba end with consonants. Most words end with a vowel. When the Limba is faced with reproducing imported words, the tendency is to give them a noun class first and foremost, and then either insert a vowel between consonants or add a vowel to the last consonant. Eg.
Pen - kupɛni
Pan – impaani/paani
Cup – hukɔɔpi-or cɔɔpi (hupɔɔthi in Safroko)

Where there is an imported word with two strong consonants coming in succession, the tendency is to insert the vowel **i** or **u** between them and add the same vowel to the final consonant. Trit in Krio becomes **tiriti** in Limba, bred in Krio becomes **kubiredi** , brɔda in Krio becomes **burɔda** in Limba. Note: **brɔda** is the Krio equivalent for ***brother*** in English. Recall that in Krio also, where an English word has three strong consonants in succession, the first consonant is dropped. Hence **trenja** for stranger; **trɔng** for strong; **trit** for street; **prɛd** for spread. Note also that Krio drops the **h** sound in a few English words that sound more or less the same as in krio. Eg. **ed** for head, **ebi** for heavy, **ɔni** for honey, **at** for hurt, **os** for house …

1.5 - Using (f) in place of (h) and vice versa/ alternating f with h.

Alternating the *f* and *h* sound while maintaining the same meaning.

Just like Themne alternates *s* and *sh* while maintaining the same meaning, so does Limba alternates *f* and *h* while carrying the same meaning, It is a fallacy then to say that there is no **f** sound in the Limba language. Recall the following words in Limba – *filiŋ (tongue), fati (child), foothi (mouth/lies), fira (carve), fɛra (winnow), fɛɛra (chance), fatha (strength), fura (sleep/spend a night), fora (clap/slap), fatu (Fatu), fina (Finah/call name) futha(bend/ a word), finkira (throw far off), fanande (divide/share), fɔlɛ (belly), fithiri (dusk), fanda(your father)*….Interestingly the **f** sound is alternated by an **h** sound without distorting the meaning – *hiliŋ, hati,*
Hothi (mouth/lies), hira (carve), hɛra (winnow), hɛɛra (chance), hatha (strength), hura (sleep/spend a night), hora (clap/slap), hatu (Fatu), hina (call name), hutha (bend, a word), hinkira (throw far aff), hanande (divide/share), hɔlɛ (belly), hithiri (dusk), handa (your father).

It must be noted that certain dialects constantly use the **f** sound, while others use the **h** sound. The Biriwa especially use the **h** sound, while the safroko use the **f** sound. When the different dialects communicate with each other/one another there is no speck of doubt in meaning. The confusion arises when users of the various dialects speak foreign/other languages like Krio. They do not see any difference in meaning when they call **hill** for **field**, or **hoo hoo**

7

for **foo foo**. To the native Limba speaker, the different sounds produce the same meaning. Note also that in Themne, the **s** sound is alternated with **sh** sound with no difference in meaning – **seth and sheth (house/build), sek and shek (tie), sebora and shebora, sema and shema.** The Mende juxtapose **r** and **l**, **ch** and **sh** simply because the phonemes **r** and **ch** are absent in the language. When faced with reproducing imported words with the **r** and **ch** sounds, the Mende substitute these with **l** and **sh** respectively. Eg **bled, lod, lat, Lɔbɔt** for bread, road, rat, Robert respectively; and **pikshɔ, pɔnkshɔ, kɔlshɔ** for picture, puncture, culture respectively.

CHAPTER 2

The Morphology of Limba

Section 2

2.1 Word Formation

Word formation is generally done through a combination of two or more syllables.

A few words, however, are formed without a combination. The syllable stands out alone with a full meaning of its own. Eg. Ka,ba,yi, wɔ , fɛ .e, sa,ta, miɲ, beɲiɲ

A few words also are formed by affixing/suffixing/prefixing the following sounds at the end of one syllable, or infixing them between two or more syllables. Sometimes both infixing and suffixing of these sounds occur to give meaningful words. Eg. **m, n, ŋ**

mb ɔɔ, (a knife) ntha (something), ɲdaamha (yam), mhompa (a leaf), ntuteŋ (intestines), mbaana(a banana leaf), mbapu (a camel), mp ɔyaŋ (an illness

Tone marks or vowel lengthening give words a different meaning:
Eg.   <u>sisa</u>
     Sisa/sisaa = bring/rice
     <u>yaka</u>
     yaka/yaaka = abuse/charity
     <u>danka</u>
     Danka/daanka = hook/curse
     <u>mɛti</u>
     Mɛti/mɛɛti = town/salt

Words accompanied with pictures

b - baahu (goat), bɛti (bird), banka (house)
d - deka (idol), daanka (hook)
f - feeli (egg), fufɛ (bat), footi (nest)
h - hɛlima (table spoon), hiyo farma (rainbow)
k - kothoro (lizard), kɔsa(pig), kɔɔsɛ (horn)
l - lantha (root), laathu (sling), liima (file)
m - manaŋ (cow), manimpire/makayoŋ (oranges)
n - ninkire (calf)
p – pinkari (gun)
r - rɔgba (hide),ronko(ronko cloth)
s – soo (horse), sosa (star), sinki (porcupine)
t – taati (bush cow), tali/tɛni (medicine)
w – wɔkita (push),wokɛkɛŋ (snake)
y - yaari (cat), yɔɔnkɔ (chameleon), yɔnkɔ (hand)ŋ -
ŋ - ŋathɛy (feet), ŋayeŋ (wood/sticks/trees)
gb – gboŋa (road), gbɔsi (axe)
th - thɛɛ (fowl), (ku) theŋ (dog)
nd - ndaamba (yam), ndoo (yes)
mb - mbompa (leaf), mbɔɔ (knife), mbapu (camel)
nt - ntutɛŋ (intestines)
nth - nthobo (raffia), nthonaŋ (sickness)
nk - nkothi (a track in the bush), nkoyo – throat; nkɔnti - neck

CHAPTER 3

Limba Grammar

Section 3

3.1 - Nouns

The Limba language, like most Nilo-Saharan languages, including Themne, operates on a noun class system. That is to say most common nouns are preceded or succeeded by a noun class. In other words the phoneme/syllable/noun class is attached to the root word or noun reference. The phoneme/noun class element could preceed, come in-between or succeed the root word. The noun class elements are either singular or plural. These include: **hu, ku, bu, mu, ma, ba, ga, g, bi, fo,ho, tho, fo, fu, ni, m, mp, n.** Generally, proper nouns and a few common nouns in the singular form stand out alone without a prefix noun class. However, common nouns in the plural form are succeeded by noun class elements, although one or two dialects have these preceded by a noun class. Eg mɛti (town), bɛti (bird), footi (nest), fothi (mouth/lie), fooya(eye), maaya(oil), bahu (goat), baakɔ (monkey), fɔɔlɛ (belly)

Singular Noun Class (NC)	Plural NC
Ku	ŋa
hu	Tha,ma,ba
wu	Mu, bi
Mb	ɛŋ, ni
Nth	ɛŋ, ŋ,
f/h'	Th'
h/f	mp

There are at least 18 noun class elements in Limba and these are either singular or plural.

ni, iŋ, ɛŋ as plural suffixes

11

mbɔɔni = knives

buyni = fires   = fires   *iŋ

mandiŋ   = waters   *bu … ni

mɛndɛŋ = days   *iŋ

ma (noun class) = too many to count, or showing liguids
huyaba, thayaba, mayaba, = an onion; few onions;a lot of onions
respectively
maaya - oil   =   oil
mandi - water/stream   =   water
mampaŋ - wine   =   wine
maninpire/mayimbire/makayoŋ - oranges   = oranges
mabili – breast milk   =   breast milk
marɛŋ, mara, masi(ni),wasi - blood   =   blood
mayɛlen, mayɛyni, malɛlen - mucus   =   mucus
mathɛni/mathɔyni - spittle   =   spittle
mapapiren/ matapiren - sap   =   sap
             =   sap
mayampɛŋ, mampɛŋ - urine   =   urine
mamehiyan - sweat   =   sweat
 **hutɔŋɔ - honey (an exception)

Ba – NC prefix showing doer of an action

Doer of an action (ba is prefixed to the verb)		
bathari	=	a runner
bakɔndi	=	a counter
bayɔli	=	a farmer
baleŋ	=	a follower
bakaŋ	=	a dancer
bapili	=	a healer/doctor

Saa - (come   Sa – (will not)
Kaa - (go)   Ka – (at, to, there)
Doo - (here)

Dondo – (here at this place)
Ba (when separated from the root word means: **do not**

Ba (before the verb) - do not
Ba (when used as noun prefix) means – doer of an action

3.2 - The Articles in Limba

The definite article is formed by adding a suffix to the root word i.e-
NC + noun (Root word) + suffix. The Suffix NC is put in the
refined form of the NC prefix to match. Eg.
Hulɔnkɔ haŋ – the hand
Thalɔnkɔ thaŋ/thɛnkɔ thaŋ – the hands.The indefinite article has
the prefix attached to the root word only – eg hulɔnkɔ; tha lɔnkɔ
yɔnkɔ haŋ, thankɔ/thɛnkɔ thaŋ – is Tonko and Sella preference

Indefinite article	Definite article
Hulɔnkɔ - a hand	Hulɔnkɔ haŋ - the hand
Thalɔnkɔ - hands	Tha lɔnkɔ thaŋ/thɛnkɔ thaŋ - the hands
Maaya - oil	Maaya maŋ - the oil
Mandi - wáter	Mandi maŋ - the water
Mandiŋ - waters/rivers	Mandiŋ maŋ - the waters, rivers
Mbompa – a leaf	Mbompa kiŋ – the leaf
Bompɛŋ - leaves	Bompɛn buŋ
Ndaamba – a yam	Ndaamba kiŋ – the yam
Ndaambɛŋ - yams	Ndaambɛŋ kiŋ – the yams
Nthonaŋ – an illness	Nthonaŋ kiŋ – the illness
Mpende – millet	Mpende kiŋ – the millet
Mafɛŋ – breath, life	Mafɛŋ maŋ – the breath, the life
Masandeŋ - needle	Masandeŋ maŋ - the needle
Kupɛni - a pen	Kupɛni ko - the pen
ɲapɛni - pens	ɲapɛni ɲaŋ - the pens
Kuyeŋ - a tree.stick	Kuyeŋ ko - the tree/stick
ɲayeŋ - trees/sticks	ɲayeŋ ɲaŋ - the trees
Bayeŋ - many trees	Bayeŋ baŋ - the trees

Fooya - an eye	Fooya haŋ - the eye
Thaaya - eyes	Thaaya thaŋ - the eyes
Baahu - a goat	Baahu woŋ - the goat
Baahuiŋ - goats	Baahuiŋ be/beŋ - the goats
Bɛti - a bird	Bɛti woŋ - the bird
Bɛtiiŋ - birds	Bɛtiiŋ be - the birds
Baakɔ - a monkey	Baakɔ wo/woŋ - the monkey
Baakɔni - monkeys	Baakɔni be - the monkeys
Foothe - a tortoise	Foothe wo - the tortoise
Footheni - tortoises	Footheni be - the tortoises
Mɛti - a town/village	Mɛti maŋ/baŋ - the town/village
Mɛtiiŋ - towns/villages	Mɛtiiŋ maŋ/baŋ - the towns/villages
Kɔsa - a pig	Kɔsa wo/woŋ - the pig
Kɔsɛŋ - pigs	Kɔsɛŋ be/beŋ - the pigs

Note that **Wo** is a suffix Noun Class in the singular form, and **be** is used for the plural form for animals, persons. The NC when used as suffixes in this case stand out alone.

The definite article in Limba comes after the noun. The definite article is formed by using the initial **mb-kiŋ** element of the word noun class and adding another sound.

Kusala ko/koŋ - the hoe   ŋa sala ŋaŋ - the hoes

Kuthodo koŋ -the mortar   ŋa thodo ŋaŋ - the mortars

 Wupithi wuŋ - the wearing   Mupithi muŋ - the wearings

 Wutɔhi wuŋ - the sewing   Mutɔhi muŋ - the sewings

Husomba haŋ - the pot   thasomba thaŋ - the pots

Hutala/huta/taa haŋ - the palm tree   tha tala/ taa thaŋ

* sumbu wo - the grasscutter(farm pest) sumbuiŋ be - the grass cutters.

* kusumbu - a long stick used for hunting grass cutters

* Kusumbu - also when witches enter into grass cutters to destroy their victims' rice farm through witchcraft

* hati wo/hatoɲ - the child   mpati muɲ/mpati be - the
children
* yɛrɛmɛ wo/woŋ - the wife/woman   yɛrɛmɛɲ be/beŋ - the
women/wives
* sɛnkɛlɛ wo/woŋ - the moon/month   sɛnkɛlɛɲ be - the
months
* sosa wo/woŋ - the star   sosɛɲ be/beŋ- the stars
* Yala baɲ - the hammock/nets   yalɛɲ baɲ - the
hammocks/nets
*yaba baɲ - the shirt/dress   yabɛɲ baɲ - the shirts/dresses
*yankira baɲ - the shorts/trousers   yankirayɲ baɲ - the
shorts/trousers
*kupahu ko - the shorts/trousers   ɲa pahu haɲ - the
shorts/trousers
*mbompa kin - the leaf   bompa/bompɛɲ buɲ - the
leaves
ntutɛɲ kiɲ - the intestines

Few nouns in Limba do not have a word class. A few borrowed
words too do not have a prefix noun class.

Eg. Banka (house), mɛti (town/village), mɛɛti (salt), sisa(cooked
rice), sukulu (school), sandeɲ/bokari (headtie)

3.2.1 - bɔsɔm baŋ / kabilɛ wo / kubɔri ko = The Family

Kafaŋ haŋ/kakutɔŋ ko - to the father's side
mbemba (ka mbemba) - predecessor/ancestors
Ka nanda (on your mother's side)
Ka kusegbe ko - on the breast milk/mother's side)
Monda - your grand mother
Ka hu mondiya -on the grand mother's side
Mbari - uncle
Nthɛnɛ - aunt
Mbariŋ - my uncle
Mbarinda - your uncle
Mbarindeŋ - your (plural) uncle

Ka hu nandiya - on the mother's side
Ka hu fandiya - on the father's side
Hu wɛndiya - brotherhood/sisterhood
Bapapa - an adult man
Bayaapa/wathe (man/boy)
Kayba/wathe - boy /man)
Bi yɛthɛ - men
Yɛrɛmɛ - woman/wife/female
Naalo (girl, female)

3.2.2 - Some conjugations

Faŋ/ Faŋ mu - my father
Fandaŋ - my father
Faantu/fandantu - our father
Fandeŋ - your father
Fandameŋ - their father
Bifanda - your father and brothers, or uncles
Naamu/nandaŋ - my mother
Nanda - your mother
Nandama - his/her mother
Naantu/nandantu - our own mother
Nandeŋ - your (Plural) mother
Nandameŋ - their mother
Binanda - your mother and her rivals, or your aunts
Wɛŋ/wɛŋ mu/wɛndaŋ - my brother/sister
Wɛnda - your brother/sister
Wɛndama -his/her sister/brother) could also mean fondly **my brother/sister** (name withheld
Wɛɛntu/wɛndantu - our brother/sister
Wɛndeŋ - your brother/sister
Wɛnda meŋ - their own brother/sister
Mbɛnda - your siblings
Mbɛndaŋ/ Mbɛnuŋ /mbɛɛmu - my brothers/sisters
Mbɛnda meŋ - their brothers/sisters
Bifandaŋ - my fathers, including uncles
Bifandantu - our fathers, including uncles, elders

Bifandama - his/her fathers, including uncles, elders
Bifanda - (1st person) your fathers, including uncles, elders
Bifandeŋ - your fathers, including uncles, elders
Bifandameŋ - their fathers, including uncles, elders

Among the Limba, the title papa/mama are used commonly when addressing/referring to the filial father/mother as well as uncles, aunts/mother's rivals/mates. **Nna** refers to the filial mother as well as aunt or elder woman. Papa refers to filial father as well as uncles/elderly men.

Wɔ/wa - a person/someone/somebody
Wɔmɛti/wamɛti - a person/mortal man) could also mean a kind person
Bi - is the plural prefix with a subtle change in the root word.
Biya - persons/people
Biya mɛti - human beings; - Could also mean kind people.

3.3 - Pronouns

Yaŋ - I
Yi - you
Wundɛ/ndɛ – he/she/it
Miŋ - we
Beŋ - you
Bindɛ – they

Ya ma, Ma/niŋ, muŋ, biŋ, mina – syllables/noun class that come after the verb (often modified) to show the object of the noun. It points out an action done to the object.
Eg. Seya ma/niŋ - come, take him/her
Seya biŋ - come, take them
Seya mina - come and take us
Tharita ma/niŋ - run away with him/her
Sɛkitha yama - take me/choose me

17

When the pronoun/noun class comes before the verb (modified) the meaning is **looking forward to** or expecting an action to be performed on the noun/pronoun.

Yama sɛkitha - I am being taken/I am to be picked up/chosen

Yi na kata - you are being carried/ taken to

Ndɛ na sɛkitha - s/he is being taken/ is to be taken/chosen

3.3.1 - Proper Nouns

Ba – this prefix is used in referring to common nouns/the trades

Bayɔli/badungbu - a farmer

Bafiri - a wood carver

Bakurɛ - a blacksmith-

Badɔɔri - a witch doctor, sorcerer

Balenki/bamandi/babɛrɛ - a diviner/a soothsayer

Badonso/badaŋ - a hunter

Bagbali - a scribe, a writer

Mathurɔkɔ/yakali - Music and dance/celebration

Bakaŋ - a dancer

Bafaŋ - a drummer/a player

Basɔŋ - a singer

Batutɛŋ - one who plays the kondi

Babaŋ - one who plays the band/drum

Bakonkoma - one who plays the konkoma

Bathamba - one who plays the hand drum

Ba'nkali - one who plays the kelen.

Bathuthu - one who blows the horn

Babulɔ - one who plays the calabash/violin

Basaaka - one who plays the shegureh

basuŋ - one who plays the bondo drum, also one who plays the small kelen.

Bamandi - one who fetches water.It also means a soothsayer

---**Ba** – when the noun class **ba** is placed after the pronoun and followed by the verb modified, ie Noun/Pronoun + ba + V - the meaning is Noun/Pronoun is to be ---

baŋ is the plural form for **ba.** The prefix is used as a gentle command showing negation. Eg. Ba thari - do not run.

When **ba** is attached to the noun, the meaning shifts to **doer of the activity/noun**. Eg. Bathari - a runner; badungbu - a farmer

When **ba** stands out separately from the verb, the meaning is the negative form, a gentle command - do not. Eg. Baluku - do not tie; bakati – do not carry/take to

a – this is a prefix meaning **to** - It denotes the infinitive form of the verb.

Eg. Agbali - to write; akaŋ - to dance;anine -to sleep; amahi - to brush; ayɔli - to plough; athari - to run; awɔlɔ - to lie down/go to bed; apiti - to wear; asimɔkɔ - to remember; awɔti - to fall down; asɛkɛthi - to take; adɛŋ - to put down/to marry; apɛthi – to wear; akati – to take to; aduteki – to return; athathi – to go down/go to the farm,work place; atali – to lay down; akeŋ - to jump, to fly; amali – to jump; ayɔli – to strive (an idiom in Tonko,Sela)

3.3.2 - Infinitive nouns

Hu - infinitive form of the noun –
Hutuka - death
Huboka - death anniversary (aboki – to weep/cry)
Huyɔla - farming
Huseri - message
Humɔnɛ - poverty/laziness
Hupanka - poverty/lacking

3.3.3 - Possessive nouns

Prefix + Ka = owned by/for
Noun/Pronoun + ta = owned by (The Safroko Limba use this)
N/P (Ma) + ka – liquid owned by/for (note – ma is a prefix/syllable for liquid)

NP (Ma) + ta - used by Safroko Limba meaning liquid, owned by/for (**note** – *ma* is a prefix/syllable for liquid)
Kupɛni ko ka Abu - Abu's pen (literally translated – a pen owned by Abu
Kupɛni ko ta Abu - Abu's pen (Safroko)
Yaba baka Abu - abu's shirt
Yaba bata Abu - Abu's shirt
Mandi maka fatu - Fatu's water
Mandi mata fatu - Fatu's water
Maya maka dora - Dora's oil
Maya mata dora - Dora's oil

3.4 - Verb Formation

Yan ma - I am - ya ma yaŋ			ma (na) am	yaŋ tɛ	(I am not,will not)
Yi na - You are-	-	yi		na	are
Wunde/nde na - she/he is is	-	(wu) ndɛ		na	
Min na - we are	-	miŋ		na	are
Ben na - you are (pl)	-	beŋ		na	are
Binde na - they are	-	bindɛ (biŋ)		na	are

Athari - to run
thara - run (a subtle command)
tharita - run away with

Negatives -- **tɛ** - not); **sa** - will not; **ba** - do not; **ta** - is not
These elemants may come before or after the verb
-------**ba** thari - do not run --- baŋ thari - do not run (plural)
ba tharati -Don't runaway with; baŋ tharati (plural)
yaŋ tɛ/ yaŋkutɜ - I am not
wundɜ se ta - s/he will not come

20

Ba stands out alone when showing a negative command

Negative command (**ba** stands out alone)
ba thari = do not run
ba kɔndi = do not count
ba yɔli = do not farm/do not strive
ba leŋ = do not follow
ba kaŋ = do not dance

a –denotes doing an action/ a task. It also means a gentle command abiye (to wash/have a bath), aloki (to wash/clean/cleanse), agbɔki (to scrub), akaŋ (to dance/ to burst), afaŋ (to hit/ to beat), asɔŋ (to sing), alɔsi (to draw/pull), apithi (to wear), aluyɛ (to hear), anɛki (to look/observe), adethi (to look/observe) athɔnthɔŋɔŋ (to ask), abili (to wear/to enter), akɔri (to kill), asɛkɛthi (to take), adagbi (to beat/flog), agbuduŋ (to beat/flog), athapi (to beat/flog),abereŋ (to cry), amase (to help), apiiti (to forget), asimiŋ (to remind), amɛy (to answer), abuuhuu/athanthiye (to deny) , ani kuyeli (to advice, give a warning).

a is prefixed to a verb to show the infinitive form
athimio - to like/love
athimiyo - to be liked/loved
ahimiyo - loved one
athambo - to hate/dislike
athambiyo - to be hated/disliked
ahambiyo - hated/disliked one

Ta is placed after the verb to show a negative action
Thimiyo **ta -** not loved/liked
Thambiyo **ta** – not hated

hu – a prefix for abstract noun
Eg- humɔnɛ - poverty
hugbaŋ/Hariyeke - wealth
hukagbaŋ - ingratitude

21

Hukampara/hunaŋ - jealousy
Hudoɔŋɔ/kuyɛnti - marriage
hudanka - wickedness
huthaniya - learning
hupanka - poverty/lacking...

Ma – is also used for the same purpose in a few words. Generally, this prefix denotes manner of--
madɔŋɔ- marriage/living together
mathaani – learning

Ka – ka is prefixed to the name of the place- meaning at/to that place - It does not stand out alone
Kamɛti - to town
Kabo - to Bo
Kabumbaŋ - at/to Bumban
Kamakeni - at/to Makeni
Kamagburaka - at/to Magburaka
Kakambia - at/to Kambia
Kakɛnɛma - at/to Kenema

Kaa – when the vowel **a** is lengthened, the meaning shifts to the verb form meaning -   go --- a subtle command
Kaa kamɛti - go to town
Kaa kabo - go to Bo

Kaye ka Bo - go towards Bo
Kata ka fatu ka - take to Fatu
Kate ka fatu ka - take towards Fatu
Seye ka Bo - come towards Bo

Kaa ba – does not want to---
Ndɛ kaa ba ka - he/she/it does not want to go
Iŋ ka ba kaa - you do not want to go
Bindɛ ka ba kaa - they do not want to go
Miŋ ka ba thɔma - we don't want to eat
Yaŋ ka ba kɔthɔ - I don't want to know

Kaba - put on airs, proud, surprise (it is also a name given to a male)
Thakaba - surprise (it is also a name given to a male)

3.4.1 - Verbs and Idioms

Atɛɲ/asarande - enough, to arrive
Wuɲ tɛɲ - it is enough, it has arrived, it has reached
e + have/has Noun/Pronoun + verb (modified) is used in the question form
e 'n tɛɲ ? e 'ɲ sarande? - Have you arrived?
e yaɲ tɛɲ? E yaɲ sarande? - have I arrived?
e ndɛ tɛɲ?/sarande? - has he/she arrived?
e miɲ tɛɲ? - have we arrived/ are we enough?
e beɲ tɛɲ? - have you (pl) arrived/ are you enough?
e bindɛ tɛɲ? - have they arrived/ are they enough?
e wuɲ tɛɲ ? Has it come? Is it enough?
e bindɛ fuɲande/sarande ? Have they reached? Are they up to the number?
Tɛɲ - means come, arrive, enough, reach

Sa and **ba** - Prefixes/suffixes showing negation

Sa - comes after N/P followed by noun
Ba - comes before verb (so modified)
Ba kay - do not go
Ba se - do not come
Ba yaki - do not abuse

+++ Sa faɲ - will not hit/beat musical instrument
Sa tuku - will not die
Tɛ/kutɛ comes after Noun/Pronoun meaning <u>not</u>
Yaɲ tɛ / yaɲ kutɛ - I am not
Yi tɛ /yi kutɛ - you are not
Ndɛ tɛ/ndɛ kutɛ - s/he is not
Wuɲ tɛ/wuɲ kutɛ - it is not

3.5 - Adjectives

Adjectives come after the nouns they describe. Adjectives too follow the noun class pattern.

Wu, ho, ko, wo ---- thurɔy (it is short) - after the noun
" " "thɔkiyɛ, thɔkuwɛ – is tall/is long

" " Bɔlɔy, black, blue
" " "fufɛ - White
" " "pothɛ -red, yellow, orange, violet
" " " fawu - grey
" " "fifiŋ - green
" " "sɛnkrɛ -multi-colour/checkered.

ŋa, tha, be, ba, ma lɔhɔy – they are fine (the plural form)

When we want to be specific, emphatic, kind of the definite article form, the preceeding noun class is refined in the appropriate form and also put at the end of the adjective. Eg wo pothɛ – he/she is fair in complexion, it is red

Wu bɔlɔy – it is black	Wu bɔlɔy wuŋ – the black one
Wo bɔlɔy – he,she, it is black	Wo bɔlɔy woŋ – the black one
Wo fufɛ – it is white	Wo fufɛ woŋ – the white one
Be fufɛ – they are white	Be fufɛ be – the white ones
Ko pothɛ – it is red	ko pothɛ ko – the red one
ŋa pothɛ – they are red(inanimates)	ŋa pothɛ ŋaŋ – the red ones
Wu fufɛ – it is white	Wu fufɛ wuŋ – the white one
Tha thurɔy – they are short(inanimates)	Tha thurɔy thaŋ – the short ones
Be thurɔy – they are short	Be thurɔy beŋ – the short ones
Ho kɔndɔkɔy – it is bent	Ho kɔndɔkɔy haŋ – the bent one
Tha kɔndɔkɔy – they are bent	Tha kɔndɔkɔy thaŋ – the bent ones
Mu thumbɛ – they are	Mu thumbɛe muŋ – the

24

straight(inanimates)	straight ones
Mindo pethɔy – we are well	Mindo pethɔy be – we that re well
Mindo kaho – we are tired/fed up with	Mindo kaho be – we that are tired/fed up
Mindo thamɔy- we are tired, not able to	Mindo thamɔy be – we that are tired---
Mindo bɔlɔy- we are black (we blacks)	Mindo bɔlɔy be – we that are black
Bendo pethɔy – you are well	Bendo pethɔy be – you that are well
'ndo wɔlɔy – you are lying down	'ndo wɔlɔy wo – you the one that is lying down
Ndɛ wo gbasɔy – he/she is tatooed	Ndɛ wo gbasɔy wo – he'she that is tatooed
Binbe kɔy – they are standing	Bindɛ be kɔy be – they the ones that are standing

3.5.1 - Mataraŋ/MathƆlintande/mathƆyintande - Adjectives

abɔy - big
athahɔ - small
abukulu - fat
amɛɛsi - small
amɛlɛsi, athahiyo - very small
alɔhɔ/ayɔhɔ - fine, good, beautiful
alɔhiyɔ - very fine
alɔhitande/ ayɔhitande - very fine/beautiful

In forming adjectives, the prefix **hu,wo,wu,ko, be,ho** – stands out alone and the descriptive word follows with slight modification.
Wo lɔhɔy - he, she, it is fine, good
Wu lɔhɔy - it is good, fine
Ho/ko lɔhɔy / yɔhɔy- it is fine, good
Hubilo ho thahɔy - the door is small
Hubilo ho bɔlɔy haŋ - the black door (referred to)

25

Be lɔhɔy - they are fine, good

ŋa lɔhɔi - they are fine, good (inanimate things, body parts)

Tha lɔhɔi - they are fine, good (inanimate things, body parts)

Ba lɔhɔy - it is fine (also too many to count) bananas--

Ma lɔhɔi - it is fine (for liquids generally) also too many to count

Note the use of **y in place of l** by the Sela and Tonko - ayɔhɔ (fine) and biyo (door)

Wo,ko, wu,ho bukulɛ - he/she/it is fat,big

Be, ba, ma, tha, ŋa bukulɛ / bukuyɛ - they are fat (The prefix selected depends on the noun class of the object referred to)

Thɔŋ/gbeŋ – self/very self/the very thing (used for emphasis). These syllables are suffixes placed immediately after the noun they qualify

Yaŋ gbeŋ na bilɛ - I, my very self own it

Yi gbeŋ bilɛ na - your very self own it

Ndɛ gbeŋ bilɛna - she/he, her/his very self own it

Thɔŋ – also means law/regulation.

Haniŋ - every - **haniŋ** precedes the noun it qualifies

Haniŋ wa/wɔ - everybody

Haniŋ hati - every child

Haniŋ ntha - everything

Wumɔ wumɔ - any one/ everyone/whoever

Kamɛ kamɛ - every where/any where

Bamɛ bamɛ - whatever/whichever

Kumɔ kumɔ - whichever

Timɛ timɛ - whatever quantity, every time, everyday

Timɔ timɔ - everyday, whatever amount/quantity

Timo tima - everyday

Nthaa yo ntha - anything

Nthaa yo ntha ka - nothing whatsoever

Nthaa ka - nothing available

Bay ka - no problem

Maaya ka - no palm oil

Wɔka - nobody (also a boy's name)

Biya ka - no persons/people

Mandi ka - no water

Note the use of **ka** – It stands out separately after the root word to show the negative (not/nothing). When **ka** is used in front of the root word, it denotes places –towns, villages, countries. It also shows directions or prepositions.

Kabumbaŋ - at/to Bumban
Kakono -at/to Kono
Kamɛti - at/to town
Kadungbu - at/to the farm

3.5.2 - Matharaŋ/mathɔlintande – Description/Adjectives

Mapothi - redness/fair skinned, also mauve, yellow
Mabɔlɔ - blackness, also green, blue
Mafufu - whiteness, also greyness
Fifiŋ – green
Mafawu - grey
In describing nouns/pronouns the noun class is put before the adjective with modification. Eg **wo pothɛ** - he/she is fair complexioned. Also,the animal is red skinned. Wu pothɛ - it is red.it is ripe
Wo bɔlɔy - he/she/it is black, also blue, green for inanimates
Wu bɔlɔy - it is black, blue, green
** apoothi - to be dirty (in Sela and Tonko); to pluck off palm nut fruit (Biriwa and safroko)

3.5.3 - Mabiliyande/hubiliyande - relationships
Abilɔ/hubilɔ - to own/to belong
Mabilɔ/mabiyɔ - ownership
Babilɔ / babiyɔ - owner
Ba bilɔ - to own (note that the root word is detached from the prefix when the infinit verb form is used)
Ya ma bilɛ/yaŋ bilɛ na/yaŋ na bilɛ - I own (the person/thing/animal)

27

3.5.3.1- Prefixes denoting possession – Possessive Nouns

Yaŋ bilɛna - I own
Ya ma bilɛ - I own it (I am the owner)
Ya ma bilɛ/yaŋ bilɛ na/yaŋ na bilɛ - I own (the person/thing)
Iŋ bilɛ na - you own it
Yi na bilɛ - you own it (you are the owner)
Wu(ndɛ) na bilɛ - she/he/it owns it
Miŋ na bilɛ - we own it
Miŋ bilɛna - we own it (we are the owners)
Beŋ na bilɛ/ Beŋ bilɛ na - You (Pl) own it
Bindɛ na bilɛ - they own it
Biŋ bilɛ na - they own it/they are owners
Mabilɔ / mabiyɔ means ownership
Note the use of **y** by Sella and Tonko

3.5.4 - Amplifiers – amplifiers come after the adjectives, just like the adjectives come after the nouns.

Repeating of words (adjectives, adverbs) for emphasis or as amplifiers
Yako - quick/fast
Yako yako - very fast
Hanthe - once/one
Hanthe hanthe - once in a while/ doing sth.slowly, without rushing
Wunthe wunthe - very few
Ka wunthe wunthe - one by one/one to each/one after the other
Ka bile - in twos
Ka bile bile - in twos/two by two/two to each
Yako yako - very quick
Timo tima/ timɔ timɔ - everyday/every time
Lɛmpu - quick/fast
Lɛmpu lɛmpu - very fast/quick
Toke - briskly
Toke toke - very briskly
Na yona yona - restless, fast movement
Na koro koro - very clearly (Koro koro – also means broad beans in Tonko)

thɔthɔdɔ - very near
kɔri kɔri – clandestine movement; not cheerful
fɔsɔyɔ - worried,place in shambles
fakasaŋ - worried
fifthi - fuggy, doubtful
fadi - fast
fadi fadi - very fast
wumo wuma/wumɔ wumɔ - anyone/whoever
bimɔ bimɔ - everyone/whichever/whoever
kamɛ - where
kamɛ kamɛ - everywhere/anywhere
timɛ - how much/how many
timɛ timɛ - everyday/every time,whatever amount/quantity
timo tima - everyday/every time,whatever amount/quantity
namɛ - how
namɛ namɛ - anyhow
haniŋ wɔ - everyone
damiŋ wɔ - everyone
hali - none
hali hali - none at all
kawunthe wunthe - one by one, one each
kabile bile - two by two, two each
hanthe hanthe - one each/ seldom/ slowly.(Cf Krio language - one one, two two)
Note - words are repeated for amplifiers of adverbs of time and manner

=====

Wo bɔlɔy **na kidɔ** - he/she/it is jet black
Wo fufɛ **na pɛrɛrɛ** - white as snow/very white
Wo pothɛ **na pɛsi** - very fair in complexion (literally, he/she fair, very fair)
Wu thɔnkɔy **na piti** - very bad, very ugly
Wu thɔniyɛ **na lɔgbɔ** - it is very wet
Wu mɛthɛ **na gbaraŋ** - it is very clear/clean
Na gberekethe - very clear, very bright, quite open, transparent

Na yɔyŋ - cool
na yondeiŋ - very cold
na wayŋ - very hot
na wunkaŋ - warm/hot
na wɔmpirɔŋ - lukewarm
na yɛ - just enough
na gbɛti/na gbɛsi - exactly
nagbɛɛti/ nafɔɔrɛ,na mɛt - to the dot, to the end
na yɔli yɔli - very tall
na gbutukulu - short and fat
na lenki lenki - lanky/thin/smallish
na pɛ - full
na thuduŋ - full to the brim
na piŋ piŋ - full to the brim
na lengbeŋ - full to the brim
na yɔɔbɛ - slowly,stealthily
na fadi - fast
na fadi fadi - very fast
na kati kati - very fast
na yeŋ - quiet
na yeŋ yeŋ - very quiet
na weraŋ - clear, very clear
na mɔɔsɛ - cool temperament, despondent
na doye - cool
na yondeŋ - very cold
na toloŋ - straight
na bɛru - straight
na kɔri kɔri - withdrawn,not cheerful
na kiliŋ kiliŋ - round, oval shape
na kili kili - round/ circular
na dɔnkinsɔŋ - drowsy, unwilling
na gbɔrɔkɔthɔ - down to the ground, grounded
na gberekethe - down to the ground, grounded
na gbayŋ - fearful
na tayŋ - tipsy
na gbay gbay - sour
na wus - be scattered

na dɔiŋ - cool manner
na niye niye - sweet
na nimi nimi - sweet
na yona yona - agitated, worried
Noun (prefix+root) + ref. noun class +kiya

3.5.5 - Possessive Adjectives

Kiyaŋ - mine/ to me
Kɛnda/kanda - yours
Kɛndama/kenama - his/hers
Kɛntu - ours
Kendeŋ - yours (plural)
Kenemeŋ - theirs
Kiyaŋ ka - to my place/mine
Kɛnda ka - to yours/to your place
Kɛnama ka - to him/her; his/her (place)
Kɛntu ka - to us/to our place
Kendeŋ ka - to yours/your place
Kɛnameŋ ka - to their place/ to theirs /to them

3.5.5 - Possessive Adjectives

Kiyaŋ - mine/to me
Kɛnda/kanda - yours
Kɛndama/kɛnama - his/hers
Kɛntu/kantu - ours
Kɛndeŋ/kanden - yours
Kɛnɛmeŋ/kanamen - theirs
Kiyaŋ ka - to my place/mine
Kɛnda ka - to yours/to your place
Kɛnama ka - to him/her, his/her (place)
Kɛntu ka /kantu ka - to us/to our place
Kantu - to us
Kendeŋ ka - to yours/your place
Kenameŋ ka - to their place/to theirs
Kanameŋ ka - to their place/to theirs

31

Noun (prefix + root) + ref noun class + kiyaŋ

Adjective	Verb	Adverb (after)	
wu, wo		kuthɛgbɛ	slowly
Ko		yako	quickly
Ba		haŋ	Until/for a while
yaŋ do	(in the process of)	mauman	Now
thari	(willing to)	kenken	short while ago
ndo		yehen	Few days ago
*wo thari	He/she will run/is running	Balɔkɔ	the other day
miŋ do	We've got to	wunaŋ	Soon
beŋ do	You've got to	nɔŋ	Later
be thari	(a short while ago)		
nde, ke	At an earlier date		
do nɔ ŋ	in the act (process)of		
Kinka	have got to		
Kiŋ ba	have got to		
Kiŋ hu	would have liked to		
Kiŋ dɛ	Am/is here; would like to		
Dɛ	he is here (am here)		
Kɛndɛ	There/at that place		

In Limba, Adjectives come after the nouns they describe. Adverbs too come after the verbs they qualify,

3.6 - Preposition

Makoye - position
Ka - as preposition/showing direction
Kapothi - down - down
Kabekede - up - up, on, above
Kakay, kakɔy, kake, kakɛ – in/inside
Kathuhaŋ /thuhaŋ - over - over, across
Kathuhanka - over there
**Kathuhanka – over the water/overseas
Mahɛŋ - behind - behind
Gbenka ba - close to -by the side of
Matete (ni) - middle -between, in the middle of
malabɔ - nearby/ against
thɔthɔdɔ - very near
kilinkiliɲ/mabɛlintɔkɔ - round

3.7 - Conjunction

matɔynande
iŋ / niŋ/mɛnɛ = and   * yaŋ iŋ yi = I and you (you and I) -
--
kɛrɛ   =   but   * yaɲ ba = I've got to

3.8 – Conditional Adverbs

Mɛnɛ - if   =   if
Bana - if   =   had it been, supposing
Kinka - in the process of   =   in the act of   /
observing
kondɛ - would have
sandɛ - would not have
kaa ba - does not want to---
mbu baana - supposing

3.9 - Interjection/Exclamation

e, a, i, gbɔɔ, gbaa, mɔnɛo

e , a ,i – denotes surprise
gbɔɔ, gbaa, gbeu – denotes belittling,
mɔnɛo – denotes down playing of someone's effort

3.9.1 – Questions (Mathɔnthɔŋɔŋ)

Wu mɛ na? - which one?
Kumɛ ? - Which one?
ŋa mɛ? - Which ones (things)
bi mɛ? - which ones? Persons/things? (which one? Which ones?)
Kamɛ na? - where is it?= Where (is)
Namɛ na? - How is it? = How is --?   (Na = is it?)
Timɛ na? - How much is it? = How much? How many?
Mbɛ mu (na)? - what is it?
Mbɛ wɔ ? - who/which one?
Mbɛ ba ? – why ? = What do you--- for
mbɛ ? - Why? What?
Nka na? / Mbɛ wɔ? - Who is?
Nka na ? - who is it ? ? = Who is it?
Bimɛna? - which ones/which are they?
Mbombɛ ? - what for? Why?
Name na? - How is it? What is happening?
Mbe ho koy? - What prevails/is happening?

ba - subjective (doer of an action) eg. Bathari - a runner
ba - do not (negative verb) eg ba thaari - do not run

<u>**Ka + verb**</u> - an intended activity as if to say <u>when you get there, this is what you should do.</u>
ka maaŋ - go and greet = go greet
ka dɔŋɔ - go and sit down = go sit down (also a slight command)
ka yɔli - go and plough/strive= go plough

muthɔnkɔy - faeces (euphemistic)
mutikiŋ - faeces (vulgar)   faeces (vulgar)

When used as doer of an action, **ba** is prefixed to the verb. When used as a command in the negative form, **ba** stands out alone.

3.10 - Inflections in Limba

In inflections, the Noun Class element may preceed, come in between, or succeed the root word, depending on the meaning.
thɔŋ - have/has eaten
athɔŋ - to eat
athɔmɔŋ - to feed someone
athɔmina - to be fed by someone
athɔmɔti - to cheat, eat an infant's/someone's food uninvited
athɔmita - to be cheated of money, have food eaten up by others
athɔminɔkɔ - to feed oneself
athɔminande - to feed each other
athɔmande - to feed on each other; cheat each other, deep kissing
athomiteke - to eat alone slowly
athomeke - to eat in secret
ahɔma - eat (a gentle command)
thɔmina - feed someone (a gentle command)
thɔme - eat with hand/spoon, live on; also right hand
thomo - was/were eaten/cheated
bathɔŋ - one who eats; a cannibal
bathɔmɔŋ - one who feeds other people
muthɔŋ - food
muthɔma - food
huthɔma - food
huthome - right hand (one to eat with)
mathɔŋ - manner of eating, where to earn a living; also a masked dancer (**mathɔma** in Krio)

(b) kɔra - kill (a command), kɔraŋ - (kill (plural- a command) akɔri - to kill, hukɔra - killing; bakɔri - a killer; makɔri - manner of killing;

akɔrɔkɔ - to kill oneself; akɔrita - to have an animal/relative/child killed by another; akɔrande - to kill each other; akɔriyɔkɔ - to kill an animal/child by oneself

3.10.1 - bana, mɛnɛ ndɛ - Conditionality

Ba na - if it were, had it been
Bana yama - if it were me
Bana yama ndɛ - had it been me
Bana yina (ndɛ) - had it been you
Bana wundɛna (ndɛ) - had it been him/her
Bana miŋ na (ndɛ) - had it been us
Bana beŋ na (ndɛ) - had it been you
Bana bindɛ na (ndɛ) - had it been them

Note that **wundɛ** is shortened to **ndɛ** in rapid speech. **Bindɛ** is also shortened to **biŋ** in rapid speech.

Ba na + noun/pronoun +na = If it were the N/P or had it been the N/P

Ba na + noun/pronoun + ma/na +ndɛ

3.10.1.1 - Ba na iŋko - If Noun/Pronoun would

Ba na yaŋ ko - If I would
Ba na iŋ ko - If you would
Ba na ndɛ ko - if s/he would
Ba na miŋ ko - If we would
Ba na beŋ ko - If you would (plural)
Ba na bindɛ ko - If they would

Mɛnɛ + Noun/Pronoun + ko + v = If N/P could/would ----
Mɛnɛ iŋ ko - if N/P would/could
Mɛnɛ iŋ ko se - if you would come/ if you are coming
Mene in ko me - if you would agree/accept

3.10.2 - **Nthampo** - perhaps/maybe

Nthampo wo se - perhaps he/she is coming
Nthampo wo thɔŋ - perhaps he/she is eating
Nthampo be nine - perhaps thay are sleeping
Nthampo be thari - perhaps they are running
Nthampo mindo yɛtha - perhaps thay will choose us
Nthampo yan do dagba/thapa/thupa- perhaps I'll be flogged
Ntampo wo furu - perhaps s/he will spend the night
Nthampa wo biye - perhaps he/she is washing/perhaps he/she
would like to wash
(**furuu** means odour or breeze/storm)

3.10.3 - **Sa** follows **nthampo** to denote the negative form

Nthampo sa + verb - may not/will not + Verb
Nthampo sa - may not/will not
Nthampo sa kay/ke - may not go/ perhaps not
Nthampo yaŋ sa kay/ke - I may not go/perhaps I am not going
Nthampo yi (iŋ) sa kay/ke - you may not go/perhaps you are not
going
Nthampo ndɛ sa kay/ke - she/he may not go/perhaps s/he is not
going
Nthampo miŋ sa kay/ke – we may not go/ perhaps we are not
going
Nthampo beŋ sa kay/ke - you may not go/ perhaps we are not
going
Nthampo bindɛ sa kay/ke - they may not go/ perhaps they are not
going

3.10.4 - **Noun/Pronoun + sa + verb = N/P may not/do not + verb**

Yaŋ sa kɔthɔ - I may not know
Iŋ sa kɔthɔ - you may not know
Ndɛ sa kɔthɔ - he/she may not know
Miŋ sa kɔthɔ - we may not know
Beŋ sa kɔthɔ - you (pl) may not know

Bindɛ sa kɔthɔ - they may not know

Akɔthɔ - to know
Makɔthɔ - knowledge/knowing
Yaŋ do kɔthɛ - I know
Yaŋ kɔɔta/kɔyta - I do not know
Yaŋ ko kɔthɔ - I've got to know/ I'll know
Yaŋ ba kɔthɔ - I need to know/ ought to know

Saa - come
Saa ka - come to…
Saa ka thɔma - come to eat/come let's eat
Do - here
Dondo - here, this very place
Saa do - come here
Saa dondo – come nearer here/ to this very place

3.10.5 - Sa and ba - Prefixes/suffixes showing negation

Sa - comes after Noun/Pronoun followed by noun
Ba - comes before verb (so modified) to give a negative command/request
Ba kay/key - do not go
Ba se - do not come
Ba yaki - do not abuse/do not hire
Ba thɔŋ - do not eat
Ba thaari - do not run
Ba wɔlɔ - do not lie down
Ba sɛkɛthi - do not take
ba sulu - do not spin
ba yɔli - do not plough/farm
ba pili - do not heal
ba sɔŋ - do not sing

Sa - a syllable put before the verb to show negation – **will not**
Sa punku - is not able/will not be able
sa se - will not come
sa kutu - will not see/get

38

sa kɔthɔ - will not know (also name of boy)
sa doŋɔ - will not sit down
sa thunkuŋ - will not pay
sa luyɛ - will not listen
sɛyŋ luyɛ - they will not listen – i.e where **bindɛ** is dropped

3.10.6 - Tɛ/kutɛ comes after Noun/Pronoun meaning <u>not</u>

Yaŋ tɛ / yaŋ kutɛ - I am not
Yi tɛ /yi kutɛ - you are not
Ndɛ tɛ/ndɛ kutɛ - s/he is not
Wuŋ tɛ/wuŋ kutɛ - it is not

Ta – a syllable put after the verb (with modification) to show negation – is not able to/ not willing to = **Noun/Pronoun + Vb (modified) + ta (active verb)**
Kay ta /key ta - is not going (to go not)
Se ta - is not coming
Ndɛ se ta - he/she/it is not coming
Yaŋ se ta - I am not coming
Miŋ se ta - we are not coming
Bindɛ se ta / sey tɛŋ - they are not coming
Iŋthome ta - you are not eating
Iŋ thimo ta - you do not like
Bindɛ thimo ta / thimo tɛŋ - they do not like
Yaŋ thambo ta - I do not hate/dislike
Fatu se ta - Fatu is not coming
Amadu thome ta - Amadu is not eating
Yari e kodo kay/ke to – Yari and kodo are not going

In rapid speech, the pronoun is deleted. Only the modified verb and **ta** is heard
Thome ta - does not eat/is not eating
Wole ta - is not lying down
Kay ta/key ta - is not going
Kuy ta - does not see
Abu kuy ta - Abu does not see

Se ta- is not coming
Binti se ta - Binti is not coming
Mari fethe ta - Mari is not laughing
Kɔthɛ ta - do/does not know
Kɔɔ ta - do/does not know
Kutɔyta - is not seen
Luyɔyta - is not heard
Dɛŋɔy ta - is not married
Deŋo ta - unmarriageable

a is prefixed to a verb to show the infinitive form
Athimo - to like/love
Athimiyo - to be liked/loved
Thimiyo - loved one
Thimiyo **ta** - not loved/liked
Athambo - to hate/dislike
Athambiyo - to be hated /disliked
Thambiyo - hated/disliked one
Thambiyo **ta** - not hated

Sa – before the verb	Meaning	Ta – after the verb	Meaning
Sa se	Will not come	Se ta	Is not coming
Sa kay	Will not go	Kay ta	Is not going
Sa key	Will not go	Key ta	Is not going
Sa/Sɛyŋ kay	Will not go	Kay tɛŋ	Are not going
Sa / Sɛyŋ key	Will not go	Key ta / tɛŋ	Are not going
Sa thimo	Will not like	Thimo ta	Don't/doesn't like
Sɛyŋ thimo	They won't like	Thimo tɛŋ	They don't like
Sa punku	Is not able to	Punke ta	Is not able to
Sɛyŋ punku	They are not able to	Punke tɛŋ	They are not able to
Sa gbonkoli	Will not talk	Gbonkle ta	Do /Does not

			talk
sɛyŋ gbonkoli	They will not talk	Gbonkle tɛŋ	They do not talk
Sa lathi	Will not walk	Lathe ta	Is/are not walking
Sɛyŋ lathi	They will not walk	Lathe tɛŋ	They are not walking
Sa nii wali	Do/Does not work	Niye ta wali	Is not working
Sɛyŋ nii wali	They don't work	Niye tɛŋ wali	They are not working

<u>Take note</u>: **Sa** and **ta** as negative affixes can be used in conjugating the verb in all the three persons – singular and plural. When **bindɛ** - the 3rd person plural is dropped in rapid speech, **Sɛyŋ** replaces **sa**, and **tɛŋ** replaces **ta**

a – this is a prefix meaning **to.** It denotes the infinitive form of the verb.
Eg. Agbali - to write; akaŋ - to dance; anine - to sleep; amahi - to brush; ayɔli - to plough/to strive; athari - to run; awɔlɔ - to lie down; apithi - to wear; asimɔkɔ - to remember; awɔti - to fall down; asɛkɛthi - to take; adɛŋ - to put down/to marry; apɛthi - to open; akati - to take to/carry; aduteki - to return sth.; athathi - to go to the work place/school/farm; atali – to lay down a child/sth.; akeŋ - to fly/to plunge; amali to jump/to skip
Atheeli – to plough

a – denotes doing an action/ a task. It also means a gentle command e g.
abiye - to wash sbd/oneself; aloki - to wash sth/a dish; agbɔki - to scrub; akaŋ - to dance; afaŋ - to hit; afori – to slap/to clap; asɔŋ – to sing; alɔsi – to draw/to pull; apithi – to wear; aluyɛ - to hear; anɛki – to watch/to observe; adethi - to watch/to observe(Tonko/Sella) athɔnthɔŋɔŋ - to ask; abili - to wear; akɔri - to kill; asɛkɛthi - to take; adagbi -to beat; abereŋ - to cry; amase - to help/assist; apiiti - to

forget; asimiɲ - to remind; amɛy - to answer/to respond; abuhu/athanthiye - to deny

3.10.7 - a---+Yɔkɔ – action done to oneself/ by one self

Alathiyɔkɔ - walk by oneself without being carried or without a vehicle/bicycle/other means of transport

Athɔminɔkɔ - feed oneself

Agbɛksɔkɔ - dress up oneself/clothe oneself

Atotiyɔkɔ - cook for oneself

Akariyɔkɔ - dish for/by oneself/take a mouthful by oneself

Abohiyɔkɔ - deliver one self (woman) /receive gift in person/personally catch

Aluyɔkɔ - hear for oneself

Akutuyɔkɔ - to see for oneself (also idiom – feel the pinch)

Infinitive verb + yɔkɔ (ɔkɔ)

Asɛkɛthi - to take + yɔkɔ - for one self. Eg. **asɛkɛthiyɔkɔ** (take for oneself) **Yɔkɔ/ɔkɔ = by/for oneself.** This also means **except for**

Note that when **m** is used as a singular prefix, in forming the plural, the **m** is dropped. Cf. **mbompa** (a leaf) and **bompa** (leaves). Also **ndɔɔmbɔ (cassava leaf)** and **budɔɔmbɔ** (cassava leaves), **mpɛɛthɛ** (a potato leaf or tubers) and bupɛɛthɛ (potato leaves);nthaatha(a cassava leaf); **buthaatha** (cassava leaves) in Tonko and Sella and **buponki** in Wara wara

CHAPTER 4

Social Life

Section 4

Traditional Rites and Ceremonies

4.1 - More nouns showing social life and culture of the Limba people

Huboka - a ceremony in memory/honour of a dear ancestor

Kukaanthi - a ceremony in memory of a dear mother

Masiyaŋ - a cleansing ritual

Kuthurɔkɔ/ yakali - a play, a festivity

Mafure - a vigil/wakekeeping ceremony

Tiyɛ - a vigil of men's society

Bondoɲ - women's ceremonial dance

Thɛgbɛ - a common dance to mark a festive occasion- bondo graduation etc-

Kuthodo - a common dance among the Tonko limba

Kudɛgbɛlɛ - a rite of passage/a rite within the gbangbani society

Kɔmɔ - a rite within the male secret society

Gbongbo - a women's dance when taking a bride to her husband

Bure - initiation ceremony into men's secret society. It involves public dancing which relatives, people from other communities patronise

Gbondokali - public dancing of men's secret society which relatives, other communities patronise

Bondoɲ - women's dance/secret society

Mayɛnyɛ - girls' dance on eve of initiation into the bondo society

Pɔrɔ - Common dance for entertainment or on festive season

Bira - common dance for entertainment, for ploughing, weeding, harvesting upland rice

Mathɔŋ - common dance for entertainment, for ploughing, weeding, harvesting upland rice

Makɔlɔ - men's dance (Kɔlɔŋ is a secret society for men among the Korankos and the Kalanthuba Limba that live in Kalansogoia chiefdom in Tonkolili district)
Masande - women's dance for entertainment
Dari/Kofo - Entertainment among the Limba, a kind of secret society for young boys

4.2.1 - Musical Instruments – Muluuni

Muluŋ – musical instr ument
Hubaŋ - drum
Nkali - kelen (wooden instrumrnt)
Kɔnthɔbende - small kelen
Huthamba - hand drum put on armpit
Kontho - wooden instrument used for announcement or during men's secret society dance
Kututɛŋ - metal harp
Konkoma - gongoma
Gboroni - balangi
Yimbeni - sangba
Kubulɔ - calabash instrument
Hankulu (angle) - a metal bar in triangular shape or U shape
Kusuŋ - bondo drum
Husaaka - shegureh
Huyenkerima - obo/flute
Kuthuthu /Kurɔki - horn for announcement, wake up call, entartainment
Kulikitha - violin

Muniye wali - Farming Tools/working tools

4.2.2 - Ba (ka) huyɔla – about farming

Huyɔla - farming
Ayɔli - to farm/plough
Bayɔli - a farmer
Bayɔliŋ - farmers

Hukay/kutɛli/feli - farmland
Thɛmbu/dungbu - farm (community farm)
Kupɔsi/thuŋ/kubo - swampland
Feli - forest land
Kuboli - grassland
Amahi - to brush
Humaha - brushing
Atɔyni/athi buy - to burn
Akaari/akari - to gather burnt wood on farm
Akari - take a handful/spoonful of cooked food.
Athɛɛli/ayɔli/agbaran - to plough
Aputu/amumputu - plough on swamp
Alathi - to poddle in swamp
Apay - to broadcast-
Athuu - to plant/transplant
Hupama - scaring of birds, other animals
Apaŋ - to scare birds, other animals
Apaŋ soki - to scare birds on newly ploughed farm (broadcast rice,etc)
Apaŋ sɔkimbɔ - to scare birds on rice farm from tassle stage to harvest time
Apuruŋ - to weed
Akunku/afaki - make fence round farm, yard—
Aŋɔŋ - to harvest rice/fundi
Ananthati - carry harvested rice to stacking spot
Adɛkɛŋ - to stack rice/millet
Kugbɔɔlɔ - wooden plank for stacking crops- rice, millet, groundnuts
Hubiri - circular stacking of rice, g/nuts on the ground
Asɔkɔy - to thresh rice/cereals on foot
Afaŋ - to thresh rice/cereals using sticks
Afuku - winnow rice freshly threshed
Adutu - take home the harvested rice/cereals etc..
Kufunkuŋ - barn/store
Afɛɛri - winnow rice/cereals newly threshed
Afɛri - winnow pounded rice
Athay - to dry in the sun

45

Bafunkuŋ - storekeeper

4.2.3 - Ba kakuyeŋ - About the tree

Kuyeŋ - a tree
ŋayeŋ/bayeŋ - trees
Hudiŋ - trunk/stem
Bathala - branch
Mbompa - leaf
Bompɛŋ - leaves
Lantha - root
Lanthɛɳ - roots
Masɛnkaŋ - flowers
Huthaa/hukolon - seed
Thathaa/makolon - seeds
Kuwa - bark
Bariki/huriki - apex
hunɛɛku - pulp

4.2.4 - Bayeŋ ba pɔmpiriki/kubɔnkɛn/pɔdɔ- common trees

Ku is the prefix for trees -
Kumankoro - mango tree
Kugbandi/kupapaala - paw-paw
Kusɛɳ - locust tree
Kunimpire/kuyimbire/kukayon - orange tree-
Kupɔpɔrɔ - grapefruit tree
Kuyemani - yemani tree
Kutɛnɛ - cotton tree
Kumɛthɛ - wild tree, the back of which is used as medicine and for hardening clothes/ronko and raffia mats, etc
Kuwolo - wild tree
Kuwɔɔ - wild tree with broad leaves that grows on I V swamps. The leaves are useful for wrapping/preserving colanut. The bark is pounded or processed as medicine also.
Hutala/hutaa/taa - palm tree
tha tala/ taa - palm trees

thonko - a cluster of palm trees
Kukoknaati - coconut tree
huthiŋ - a bunch of palmnut fruits
husigbɔ - a bunch of fruits
humankoro - a mango
tha mankoro - few mango fruits
mankoro - plenty mango fruits
bamankoro - plenty mango trees

4.2.5 - Hande/hondi ------ Grass and cereals –

Hande/hondi- grass (also fande or fondi)
Paka/paga- rice
Mpende/pende- funde (millet)
Gbodoŋ/thaanki/lɔɔmba- sorghum
Thaanki – maize (corn)
Serekethe/thehiya- pearl millet
Mandɛrɛ - groundnuts

4.2.6 - Ba hutota - about cooking

Hutota - cooking (Noun form)
Batoti - a cook
Batotiŋ - cooks
Atɔrɔnti - light boiling/heating
Apooni - parboiling
Atoti - to cook rice, cereals only
Apoŋ - cook other food crops-cassava, potato, yam etc
Ayɔŋ - to pound rice, pepper, etc

4.2.7 - Munikineke - utensils

Husomba/hukɔtɔ - pot
Hukɔɔpi/hupɔthi/hugbonki - cup
Kumpa - spoon (kumpa is also an imperative verb – peel sth.)
Kutoŋ - wooden bowl (also means bread in Tonko and Sela)-
Pani/mpani - an enamel bowl/dish

47

Mbɔɔ - knife
Hurinki - firestone
Tharinki - fire stones
Sugbu - hearth/fireplace
Fɔɔtɔ/mafɔɔtɔ - ashes
Kubilo/ kupɛɛpɛ - calabash
Laiyaŋ - a metal pan used as bowl for drawing water from a spring. It is aso used as a measuring pan.

4.2.8 - Ba Nthonaŋ/mbomaŋ – about Illness

Nthonaŋ/mbomaŋ - Illness
Nthonani/mbomani - illnesses
Huthara/hupassa - diarrhoea/ running stomach
Hubɔta/hukasa - vomiting
Nsekɔ/nseku - hicupping
Kudondi/hɔlɛ ho mandi - dysentry
Mawɔdɔyŋ/siraboli - malaria
Fɛthɛgbɛ - measles
Kubaakɔ/mbakɔ - convulsion
Makɛndɔyŋ - fit/epilepsis
Bapili/bapuyu - medicine man/woman, healer, doctor
Balenki/bamandi/balɔlɔn/babɛrɛ- a sorcerer/soothsayer
Bamuyma/bahuyuŋ - midwife/TBA
Mawuru - a swelling
Huthema - a boil
Thathema - boils
Husɛsɛ - groin
Kusii/kupiiyo/kupintaŋ - dizziness
Hubɔkɔrɔ - goiter
Hugbogbo - noddle
nkɔdɛ - hiccup
mutheke - scabies
kɔrɔsi - gonorea

4.2.8.1 Ebola

A strange disease that killed above 3,500 people - men, women and children - in Sierra Leone between May 25, 2014 and September 2015. The Ebola Virus Disease entered Sierra Leone through Kailahun District around the Koindu area which borders with Guinea where the EVD started in March 2014. Koindu also borders with Liberia.

The EbolaVD is transmitted through physical contact with the body fluids of the sick person, the clothes or beddings that the sick person uses, touching the body of the sick person, washing the dead body of the person who died of the EVD.

The EVD spread from Kailahun and Kenema Districts, the first Epicentres, to every district in the country including Freetown - Western Urban and Western Rural Districts. The last epicentres were in Western Area (Freetown), Port Loko and Kambia Districts.

4.2.9 - Ba Malɔkɔ maŋ/lɔkɔ ban – about the time/date –

Adverbs of time

Malɔkɔ maŋ - the time/date
Malɔkɔ - day/time
Mandɛŋ/mɛndɛŋ - days
Mathinki - second/ a wink of the eye
Sibiri - minute
Madɔŋɔ - hour
Gbɛŋ - whole day
Kudu - whole night
Piri-piri - all night
Sankaa - morning
haatɛ - afternoon/day light
mafɔnkɔlɛŋ - evening
fuyɛ - night
hintima/huntuma - darkness

4.2.10 - Ba kahuyaapa/kahuwatheya – about manhood/men's secret society

Bure/kugbɛkɛti - men's society. The initiation ceremony for boys is observed once in every five/ten years in some communities generally. Smaller villages will converge to perform this ceremony. Others would send their boys to the bigger villages where the ceremony is observed that year.

Mayɔkɔŋ/kugbɛkɛti - public dancing by potential initiates during eve of initiation ceremony. Relatives and well-wishers in and around the host community and distant villages come to witness/participate in this event.

Thodoŋa/sakathala - old member

Gbaku - would-be initiate

Blakoro - non-initiate/ none member

Bakurɛ - the blacksmith – the "doctor"

Sesa - Assistant "doctor"

Basampɛrɛ - the mediator between the parents and the initiates

Sema - god father (attends to the welfare of the initiate)

Badiŋitɔkɔ - old member (the immediate predecessor of the new initiates)

Kunku - the hostel/domitory

Thɛnkidɛŋ - the sacred field where the MGC takes place

Naa bamba - the cook (generally a woman) for the initiates

Loŋ - a resting place for the initiates during the public dancing. Dancing normally starts from about 7.00 p m to 8.00 a.m the next day.

Alinthi ŋalahaa - dressing the would-be initiates to travel to other vilages informing relatives about date for the public dancing

Mayɔkɔŋ/kugbɛkɛti - public dancing at eve of initiation from 7.00 p m to 8.00 a.m

Tharumba - a location close to the stream where the initiates spend the day learning the tradition and culture, and the roles of adulthood.

Horonko - ceremonial gown worn by initiates on graduating from the bush school.

Bandoyŋ - This is a dress of animal skins worn by initiates during the public dance on eve of initiation. The dress is worn once and for all.

Hugbaiha - a cap made of tails of animals to match the dress above

Nthagbɛŋ - a cap decked with rubber strips to match the dress above

Yakuiŋ - shakers – made form bottle tops

Gbunduku - a short cap by canditates who have graduated from the bush school-

Kuliŋgbɔŋ - ceremonial wooden pole towering over and high above the hostel

Gbaŋgba - the spirit governing the men's society. This spirit is also called Gbangbani by those out of the tribe.

Balimbaŋ - young girl that carries her brother's luggage when visiting relatives after graduation

Akaŋ - to dance, also to burst/drill

4.2.11 - Ba ka huyɛrɛmɛ - about womanhood/women's society

Bondoŋ - the bondo society

Mayɛnyɛ/ kukanthanghan - public dance at eve of initiation day

kulathaŋ dance at eve of graduation from the bondo bush

Kulu - the dormitory/where the girls/initiates spend the night

Kuyaramaŋ - the bush school where learning and other rites take place during the day

Mayenkeeni - a fresh graduand from the bondo bush

Dɛnkɛnɛ - slow ceremonial match of initiates returning home as graduates or **mature** women

Kampa - a rite for graduating initiates to go through. This is done in secret

Badigba/barigba - head of bondo society

Sinka bondo - deputy digba ----

Naafat - assistant to the digba

Sema - god-parent/woman who attends to the initiate girl

Basema - an old member

Kuyogba - a funeral match, accompanied by a dirge. Only members participate in this ceremony

4.2.12 - Ba huwɛthɛ/huyaku - about witchcraft

Huwɛthɛ/huyaku - witchcraft

Bawɛthi/bayaku/yaku - a witch/wizard

A fina ba huwɛthɛ - to be publicly pronounced as a witch for having bewitched a child/sbd

Athembɔkɔ ba huwɛthɛ - public confession by a witch/wizard

Athembɔkɔ - confession

Babarɛ/basakapi - a medicine man specialized in investigating witchcraft through some rites

Kubare- the rite for proving some body's participation in witchcraft

Bathɛmbali - the first accused in witchcraft

Afɔsɔkɔ - to metamorphose/transform into witchcraft

Hubaana - an ingredient in proving witchcraft. The medicine man cuts down a banana tree, performs some ceremony on the babana using incantations. The ceremony is done in the evening hours. The tree is examined the following morning. When a leaf sprouts up on the cut end, it means the accused is innocent. There is much singing and dancing, and compensation for humiliation is granted. A leaf does not sprout in the banana where the person is guilty. In fact it rots! The chief would then impose a heavy fine on the guilty person, and demand compensation to the complainant or wronged family.

Bathakari - a medicine man specialized in investigating theft and other crimes using a red hot knife drawn from the blazing fire.

Kuthakari - a devise used by a medicine man specialized in investigating theft and other crimes--- A long knife is heated red hot in fire. Some slimy lotion is rubbed on the palm of the suspect/accused. The red hot iron is put on the palm of the accused. If the person is innocent, the rod/knife is cold. The person has the feeling of ice being poured on him/her. If the person is guilty, even at a distance the heat of the rod torments him/her. He/she dare not allow it to be put on the palm but admits guilty at once.

Kuthɔnkɔni/kudɔɔri- swearing/a curse

Bathɔnkɔni/badɔɔri- a specialist in invoking a curse/ swearing

Kubali/kubɛy - to be accused of sexual intercourse with another man's wife.

Masiyaŋ - a cleansing ritual

4.2.13

Ba kahudɔŋɔ/kuyɛnti – about marriage

Badɛŋ/bayɛnti/folayo- bridegroom/husband

Yɛrɛmɛ- wife

Kudeethii - betrothal

Bafuŋ - a mature unmarried girl

Alukutu thika - to virginate a girl (literally <u>tie lapa</u>)

Aluku huthuken - an engagement – to - marry ceremony (to tie cola nut literally).

Athi nahulu - paying of bride price

Woti - a rival/mate

Naati - brothers, sisters of the husband

Thɔnɔ - mother-in-law (also means wealth/riches)

Kɔmɔnɛ/kɔmɛnɛ/lahɔy - father-in-law/brother-in-law

Kupɛɛti - taking a girl in marriage

Abaŋaŋ - to reject a partner/divorce

Abariŋande - to separate/part company

Abalaŋaŋ - to flatter with another man's wife

Kuthɔmbɔ - sodomy/incest/marriage between close relatives

Huwotine - rivalry in marriage in polygamous homes

Woti - rival/mate

Biwoti - rivals/mates

Hunaati - jokes expressed between a woman and her husband's younger siblings

Naati - husband's younger brother/sister

Binaati - husband's younger brothers/sisters

Mathɔnɔ – mother-in-law, sister-in-law relationship

Thɔnɔ - mother-in-law, sister-in-law

Bithɔnɔ - mothers-in-law, sisters-in-law

Makɔmɔnɛ/malahɔy - father-in-law, brother-in-law relationship

Kɔmɔnɛ/kɔmɛnɛ/ lahɔy - father-in-law, brother-in-law

Bikɔmɔnɛ/bilahɔy - fathers-in-law, brothers-in-law

Hunaŋ/hukampara - jealousy

Banaŋ/bakampara- a jealous person

Kubɔndɔŋ- a man going to marry to the woman; a man moving into his wife's home

4.2.14 - Ba Kuthahinɛŋ ko– about the firmament/sky

Kuthahinɛŋ- sky/firmament

Kuthahinɛŋ ko – the sky/firmament

Kaŋ - sun

Sɛnkɛlɛ - moon

Sosa - star

Sosɛŋ/ŋasosa - stars
Kuyiliŋ - dark cloud
Potoyŋ - clouds

4.2.15 - Malɔkɔ maŋ gbeŋ/lɔkɔ baŋ gbeŋ- Specific time of the day/night

Sanka - morning
Sanka fithibi - very early (before dawn)
Kuputhuŋ kaŋ - before dawn around 5-6.00 am
Hutheyaŋ ho yɛrɛmɛ - around 9.00 a.m
Hutheyaŋ ho kayba/wathe - around 11.00 a.m
Kaŋ huteete - midday
Haatɛ - afternoon
Huthinkɔ ho kaŋ - around 2 o clock (breaking of the sun
Mafɔnkɔlɛŋ - evening
Pitiyɛ - dusk
Fuyɛ - night
Hintima/huntuma - darkness/dark at night
Fuyɛ tete – mid night

4.2.16 - Kolon koloni---The Weather

Potoyŋ - clouds
Thoo - hail stone/ice
Faka - cold
Nthonthoŋ - hot/hot weather
Kufefena - harmattan
Huyilimati - dark nights when the moon is not shining
Bambaraŋ - flood
Mameheyaŋ - sweat
Matheneke - shivering
Kuyiliŋ – cloudy sky
Kole – fair weather, with no rain clouds

<u>4.2.17 - Mathuŋande/makutande – meetings</u>

Bagbɔdɔ - Chairman/Chair Person
Wo lemɛ Bagbɔdɔ - Vice Chairman

Bagbaali - secretary
Bakɔsɔŋ/kɔsinɔkɔ - Treasurer/Storekeeper
Bayela - Propaganda Secretary
Bagbɛngbɛŋ - Auditor

4.2.18 - Hugbakine - chieftaincy

Gbaku - chief
Bakandɛ/bakanda/bathampi - Paramount Chief
Bathagba/basection - Section Chief
Bamɛti - town head man
Bayaha - village head man
Donkoron - region
Bompi - chiefdom
Kuthagba - section
Mɛti - town
Masothe - section in a town
Hugbɔmi - a village
Konkoso - a hamlet
Banka - house
Hubikidi - a farm hut (round)
Kubankaŋ - a farm hut bigger than above

4.2.18.1 Ma as Prefix
Ma is prefixed to the name of the chiefdom to refer to the entire chiefdom
E.g Mathɔɔnkɔ, mabiriwa, masɛla, masafrɔkɔ, masonkoŋ, mawarawara- ie. Tonko Limba, Biriwa Limba, Sella Limba, Safroko Limba, Sonko and Wara Wara Limba Chiefdoms

4.2.19 - Huthaniya/huthanuwa/mathaani - learning
Huthananiya/huthananuwa/mathanani - teaching

bathanani - a teacher
karmɔkɔ - teacher/Quoranic teacher
bathaani - a learner
karandeŋ - learner/kuranic student
karanthɛ - learning centre/school

55

bagbali - a scribe, a quoranic scholar, a secretary
**a gbaali - to write indiscriminately

4.2.20 mawali/waliŋ - trades/occupations

bawali - a worker
a sulu - to spin
basulu - one who spins
ayɔli/ba yɔla - to farm/to strive
bayɔli - a farmer
mayɔli - manner of farming
kuyɔli - farm harvest
dungbu - a farm
ba dungbu - a farmer
ba pila - to heal
apili - to heal
hupila - healing
mapili - manner of healing
bapili - a healer
husɔŋa - singing
ba sɔŋa - to sing
masɔŋ - manner of singing/singing
basɔŋ - a singer
kuluŋa/kuluŋ/kuyuŋ - a song
bathonko - a tapper of palm tree for wine/ one who taps palm trees
baŋɛli - a palmwine tapper
huŋɛla - palmwine tapping
ba ŋɛli - do not tap palmwine
hudonso/hudonsia - hunting
badonso - hunter
madonsia - hunters' dance
ba ni hudonso - do not hunt (don't do hunting)
bagbali - a writer
ba gbali - do not write
bafaŋ - a drummer/player of a musical instrument
ba faŋ - do not drum/play(also-do not hit)
baŋasi - a driver

56

hutuka - death
matuku - manner of death
atuku - to die/to be dead
wo tukɛ/batuku - the dead/has died
ba tuku - do not die
amanki - to bury
humanka - burial
bamanki - one who buries
bamankiŋ - those who bury
ba manki - do not bury
huloma - a grave
baloma - grave digger
balomɛŋ - grave diggers
baboki - a mourner
babokiŋ - mourners
Kasanke - white shroud for burial

4.2.20.1 - baŋ is the plural form for **ba.**
The prefix is used as a gentle command showing negation. When **ba** is attached to the noun, the meaning shifts to <u>doer of the activity/noun</u>. When **ba** stands out separately from the verb, the meaning is <u>the negative form</u>, a gentle command - **do not**
Baŋ manki - (you plural) do not bury
Baŋ pili - you do not heal
Baŋ yɔli - you do not farm/plough

4.2.21 - Kulombo iŋ mathɛbɛŋ – War and Peace
Kulombo - war (also in-fighting)
Balombo - a warrior/a fighter
Korogba - war lord
Kudekeli - a fight/fighting
Badekeli - a fighter
Thekere - a rebel
Pinkaari - gun
Silanhɛ - sword
Sigba - dagger
Bambadɛ - cap for warrior
Mathɛbɛŋ - peace, tranquility

Kuyaafɛ - freedom, relief
Kuyankaŋ - independence

4.2.22 - Makɔsɔŋɔŋ iŋ bakɔsɔŋɔŋ- judgement and the
judiciary/the judges
Siraani - laws
Thɔɔni - rules and regulations
Basiraŋ - a lawyer/ one who knows the law, adheres to the law.
Baseeri - a witness (**huseri** in Tonko/Sela means a message/news)
Bafuŋutu - a complainant
Kukɔsɔŋɔŋ - judgement/trial
Bakɔsɔŋɔŋ - a judge/magistrate
Gbaku - chief
Kuloho - right
Kuthonko - wrong
Kubikitha - a bet
Thɔnkɔmaseri - exhibit
Hugbɔlɔŋ - prison/jail
Huwaline - slavery
Waali - a slave
Mbaaliŋ - slaves
waali - devil
mbaaliŋ - devils
wali - work
waliŋ – works/trades/employment
mawaliŋ - works/trades/jobs

4.2.22.1 - Duniya baŋ/Kafay wo - the world (also the country)
Kɛkɛŋ ko - the world, the earth, the dirt,the country--
Baduniya - a troublesome person (an idiom)

4.2.23 - Ba ka dina - about religion
Dina - religion
Dina baŋ - the religion
Kanu Masaala - God almighty
Mariki - Lord and Saviour
Humuslimi - Islam

Hukristɛŋ - Christianity
Wukande - no religion/traditional religion
Bɛsɛ/wasi - a praying lot
Mɔɔsi - mosque
Sale - prayers (Muslim)
Ani sale - to pray (Muslim)
Kutɔyti - church
Kuraminɛ - prayer (Christian)
Ani kuraminɛ - to pray (Christian)
Abiyo/agbilisi - to be baptized
Huthenbɔɔkɔ- confession
Maleeka - angel
Sethaani - Satan
Waali wo - the devil
Laniya - belief
Balaniya – a believer
Humamande/huyenkele- a bell
Ani / athi laniya – to believe generally
Ariyana – heaven
Yahanama – hell
Bakela – Messenger
Banabi - a Prophet
Baduba – a blessed one/a saint

4.2.24 - **Mathurɔɔkɔ/yakali** – Music and dance

Bakaŋ - a dancer
Bafaŋ - a drummer/a player
Basɔŋ - a singer
Batutɛŋ - one who plays the kondi
Babaŋ - one who plays the band/drum
Bakonkoma - one who plays the konkoma
Bathamba - one who plays the hand drum
Ba'nkali - one who plays the kelen.
Bathuthu - one who blows the horn
Babulɔ - one who plays the calabash/violin
Basaaka - one who plays the shegureh

Basuŋ - one who plays the bondo drum, also one who plays the small kelen.
Bamandi - one who fetches water. It also means a soothsayer

4.2.24.1 - Temporary/Specific titles-
Baboora - a widow
Bakirɛ - a widower
Thodoŋa - a bachelor
Sonthiki - head wife
Balihaŋ - orphan
Konsa/komisa - a suckling mother/mother/parent
Bafɔɔlɛ - a pregnant woman
Bafuŋ - an adolescent girl
Bafuyuŋ - a traditional birth attendant

4.2.25 - Yikiyaani - Settlements/dwellings

Huboŋ - section
Kɛkɛŋ - ground, country, the world
Duniya - the world
Kugbagba/kuthagba - section
Donkoroŋ - region
Kubankaŋ - a farm hut
Hubikidi - a small farm hut/house
Kuresiya - a small farm hut
Banka - house
Konkoso - hamlet
Hugbɔmi - village
Mɛti - town, different from mɛɛti (salt)
Kuru kuru - small section within a village
Masoothe - small section on the outskirts of a village
Dungbu - farm

4.2.26 - Mupitha/mubiila/mugbɛksɔkɔ – dressings/clothes
Apithi/abili/athɔɔ - to wear (the verb form)
Mupithi/mubila/mugbɛkɛsi - clothes, dressings
Yaba – shirt/a woman's dress

60

Kupaahu/kuyankira/yankira/ kupɔmbɔ - trousers/shorts
Thika/karagba - a wrapper/lapa
Kufaka - cap/hat/turban
Bambadɛ - v-shaped cap
Sandeŋ/bokari - head tie
Ngbeŋ/nkele/nyenkele - bangle/bracelet
Gbanthaani/mabɔpi - earrings
Hugbanthaŋ - earring
Hubɔɔpi - earring
Mɔnki/munɔnki - beads
Kufaama - traditional men's under pants (V-Shaped).
Nthaka - traditional women's under pants – a piece of cloth
strapped round the waist with loose end at the back and front.
 Nthaka is different from **ntha kaa** (nothing)
Kudagbala/ kudagbɛɛ - shoe
Dagbalɛŋ/dagbɛɛni -shoes

CHAPTER 5

Section 1

The Human Anatomy

5.1 - Kɔtɔ ko/ku wɔmɛti - the human body
Ba kɔtɔ ko/koŋ - about the body
Huya/yaha - head
Mbɔɔlɛ - a strand of hair
Bɔɔlɛ - hairs
Huyethi/yethi - face
Huthinɛ - nose
Thinɛ - nose
Mapɛrɛŋ - nose/nostrils
Kuluha/kuyiha - ear
Konkoro - skull
Fooya - eye
Kusɔkɛ - lip
Basɔkɛ/ŋasɔkɛ - lips
Huthithi - a tooth
Thithi - tooth
Thathithi - teeth
Kunɛni - gum
Nkɔnti/kɔnti/nkoyo - neck
Nkoo - throat
Hubɛkɔ - Adam's apple
Bɛkɔ - Adam's apple (Tonko)
Kanka - chest
Kuwala - rib
ŋawala/bawala - ribs
Fɔɔlɛ/fɔɔyɛ/kotho - stomach/belley
Hukotho - stomach of an animal (Biriwa)
Huthukuma/thukma - heart
Kukɔnɛ - liver
Bakɔnɛ/ŋakɔnɛ - livers

Kufuku - kidney
Kulanki - lung
Ntutɛŋ - guts
Kugbeke - hand, the upper arm
Gbeke - hand, the upper arm
Hulɔnkɔ/yɔnkɔ - hand
Kulankaŋ - armpit
Kuwokaŋ - shoulder
Kuthenke(li) - finger
Ɲathenke(li) - fingers
Kusɛmpɛ/kusɛmbɛ - finger nail
Hunima - palm
Kuyulu - elbow
Firika - waist
Huteete - the middle ie waist
Kuyeli - eyelid
Buyeli - eyelash
Kutɔŋ - beards
Buthɔmɔti - moustache
Kondoni - whiskers
Kupuŋ - cheek
Huyɛlɛ /hulɛlɛ - leg
Kuthɛy - foot
Hugbuŋ/Gbuŋ - knee
Hothoori/huthopi - toe
Thathoori /thathopi - toes
Kulonki - lower leg
Sɔkɔrɔ - back of the neck
Hudɛɛdɛ - cerebellum
Mabenkɔ/mabuku - brain
Mgbengbeeri - spinal cord
Ɲathondo - buttocks
Mathuluŋ - marrow
Kutholi – bone
Huwori - jaw
Kupuŋ - cheek
Thawori - jaws

63

Kudekuŋ - chin
Bawori - calf
Baworiŋ - calves
Kunanka - sole
huthɔnthi - navel
nthɔnthi - umbilical cord
Huyɛlɛ-foreleg (referring to four-footed animals)
Kufaathi - hind leg (referring to four-footed animals)
Marɛŋ/masiini/mara/wasi- blood
Mandi - water
Manɛɛni - tears
Mapɛɛni - pus/mucus
Mayɛlɛŋ/mayɔyni/malɛlɛŋ - mucus
Hulɛthu - phlegm
Mafɛŋ - breath/ breathing/life
Mayampɛŋ - urine
Ayɔɔhi - to urinate
Athisile - to sneeze
Sakuyni - yawn
Anine - to sleep
Anɔnkɔri/anɔnkɔli - to snore

CHAPTER 6

Naming of Children

Section 6

6.1 Naming of Children

Among the Limba generally, most names given to children are
associated with various meanings derived from: days of the week,
months of the year, ceremonial occasions, seasons, the ancestors,
sequence of birth, events, pleas to God,witches etc.

6.1.1 - Names associated with days of the week.
Kathi - name given to a girl born on Sunday
Thɛnɛɲ - name given to a girl born on Monday
Thalaɲ - Name given to a boy born on Tuesday
Thaala - Name given to a girl born on Tuesday
(thalatha/kupaɲande)
Yaraba - name given to a boy born on Wednesday
Yalamusa/lakamusa - name given to a girl born on Thursday
Muɔa/Muɔu   name given to a girl born on Thursday
Muusa - name given to a boy born on Thursday
Yarimɛ - name given to a boy born on Friday
Yari - name given to a girl born on Friday
Simithi - name given to a girl born on Saturday

Sunkarie – name given to a girl born during the month of fasting
(Rahmadan)
Sɛɛkɛ - name given to a girl born during the month of March,
believed to be the hottest month.
Fatha - strength (a boy's name)

6.1.2 - Names associated with women's secret society (Bondo)
- sequence of initiation
Rukɔ/rikɔ - head girl among the initiates/ or the first girl to be
initiated among the batch

Yenɔ - 2nd girl
Bura - 3rd girl
Sama - 4th girl
Ndemɔ - 5th girl
Yenkeni - 6th girl

6.1.3 - Titles within the women's secret society (Bondo)
Digba - head of the society. Directly responsible for initiating girls and does the FGC)
Nafat - Assistant Digba (head)
Sinka bondo - Deputy Digba
Sampaa - a dancer close to the head of society
Bondigba - head of the old initiates (basemɛŋ)
Bɔnkaa - girl undergoing initiation
Bagboroka - non-initiate girl

6.1.4 - Names associated with men's secret society (Bure/gbangbani)

Bakurɛ - blacksmith/head of society
Sesa - deputy head of society
Sema - god parent
Borothiki - an old member
Gbaku - boy undergoing initiation
Blakoro - a non-initiate (Gborka is the themne word for blakoro)

6.1.5 - Names in sequence of birth

Sara - first born boy
Sira - first born girl
Thamba - second born boy
Kumba - second born girl
Maako - third born boy
Fina - third born girl
Fatha - fourth born boy
Finaba - fourth born girl
Lansana and Luseni - names given to male twin partners, the first and second respectively

Yemi and kɔɔtɔ - names given to male/female twin partners, the first and second respectively

Assanatu and Sɛntu - names given to female twin partners, the first and second respectively

Sayo - boy/girl born after twins

6.1.6 - Names associated with occasions, ceremonies, seasons, pleas to God or witches etc.

Yandi - Do/please spare this one at least. This is generally a girl's name. A few boys are called by this name also i.e in a situation where the mother had borne at least two or three boys who did not survive. There is the belief that by calling the boy a girl's name, the witches will mistake him for a girl. They will not harm him. He will live longer.

Beloho - You are right. I beg you. This name is given to both boys and girls

Kutuyɛn - have pity on me. At least let this one survive - a boy's name

Manika - there is no way to handle this – a girl's name

Thambo - maybe will survive / will be spared – a boy's name

Bagbon - (labour) in vain. They may not spare this again) – a boy's name.

Sama - will not (count him yet as a survivor) – a boy's name

Saman - will not (count her yet as a survivor) – a girl's name

Kute - have seen/have had – name given to both boys and girls

Malo - joy (boy born during the festive season)

Maloka - no joy (others have died before him/her, no rejoicing)

Sabu - an opportunity; middleman

Yikiban - respect

Yaapo - father's name sake (daddy)

Naawo - mother's name sake (mommy)

Thabɛn - do not expect-- (a girl's name)

Kɔnthɔn - boy born during the hunger season

Bamba - girl born when her mother served as **naa bamba** (cooked for initiates)

Thadɔma - not counted, not considered – as one fit to bear a girl

Piiti - have forgotten - a girl's name pleading with the witches to forget about her

Muuyo - Patience – a girl's name

Pɛyɛŋ - leave me alone – a girl's name

Penke - have met – a girl's name

Benkute - have you(Pl.) seen/got – name of boy/girl

Bankɔlɔ - do not bother/do not venture – a boy's name- a request for witches not to make an attempt at <u>eating</u> this one any more.

Bakay - do not go (to the world of the dead) - a girl's name

Beekay - they are going (back to the world of the dead. No hope of child surving) - a girl's name

Mbemba - male ancestor (a boy named after an ancestor)

Bande - what used to – a boy's name

Dantʰɛkɛ - an explanation, a narrative, a message – a boy's name (a boy born at a time the father had a suit.

Kunaŋ - a boy's name (giving an account)

Biyaka - no persons, no people – a boy's name

Kabiya - where there are people - a boy's name

Nɛkiyaŋ - watch on my behalf - a girl's name

Baynaka - nothing to fear

Tepeta - will not say/tell (a boy's name)

Tɛpiyaŋ - say it for me (a girl's name)

Boora - name given to a girl born after the death of the father

Palɔ - fear (a boy's name)

Nɛni/nɛniyo - a girl born during bereavement, mother shed much tears during pregnancy. Manɛni = tears)

Hɛlɛŋ - a girl's name meaning **again** (may be eaten up again, please spare her this time)

Sabena - name of boy/girl meaning (will not challenge—you people)

Sakɔtʰɔ - a boy's name meaning (may not know--- if this will be spared)

Biyaasi- name of a boy born while father was on a trip/journey

Mboompa – boy/girl (sickly – constant use of herbs/leaves for cure)

The prefix **ka** denotes places, towns, villages, countries

Ka bumban, kamabai, kabo, kamakeni, kasasi, kafadugu,

kabala, kapuyɛŋ, kakiampi, kamadina, kakambia, kalonsari, kalonke
- mountains/hills
  ka hɔmbaana (at the hill/mountain, Hombaana,
kathakɔblɔna,kasokodona

- rivers/srteams
kamabɔlɛ, (at the River Mabole) kasɛli (at the River Seli),
kamatalɛŋ,kamasumunɛ,kamathinki.......

More nouns and adverbs

6.2 - Ba Malɔkɔ maŋ/lɔkɔ baŋ – about the time/date
Malɔkɔ maŋ - the time/date
Malɔkɔ - day/time
Mandɛŋ/mɛndɛŋ - days
Mathinki - second/ a wink of the eye
Sibiri - minute
Madɔŋɔ - hour
Gbɛɛŋ - whole day
Kudu - whole night
Piri-piri - all night. Note: kupirinpiri means wall
Gbɛnkudu - an idiom, meaning - daily bread.
Wiki - week
Sɛnkɛlɛ/sɛnkɛ - month/moon
Hunina/nina - year
Thanina/thaninɛŋ - years
Bayilɔkɔ - clock (literally the one that goes round and round

6.2.1 - Malɔkɔyŋ maŋ – the days
Malɔkɔ ma ka wiki wo - the days of the week
Mɛŋ na - they are:
Kathi - Sunday
Thɛnɛŋ - Monday
Thalaatha/ kupaŋande - Tuesday
Yaraba - Wednesday
Yalamusa/lakamusa - Thursday
Yarimɛ/yumaŋ - Friday

Simithi - Saturday

Note that **maŋ** is the definite article qualifying nouns which Noun Class is **ma**
Mandi maŋ (the water); mampaŋ maŋ (the waters/rivers); manimpire maŋ (the oranges); mayaba maŋ (the onions); mathaamba maŋ (the tomatoes).

Also when **ma** is used as Noun Class prefix showing manner, or belonging to, **maŋ** is used for the definite article. Eg. Mayɔli maŋ (the manner of ploughing); madɛnki maŋ (the arrangement); matoti maŋ (the manner of cooking); makɔndi maŋ (the manner of counting/the count); malathi maŋ (the manner of walking/the steps)

6.2.2 - Sɛnkɛlɛŋ be/ sɛnkɛni be - The months
hunina haŋ/ huyina haŋ - the year
Sɛnkɛlɛŋ be/ sɛnkɛni be kahunina haŋ - the months of the year
Biŋ na - they are:
Pɔli-pɔli - January
Bankile wo yɛrɛmɛ - February
Bankile wo wathe/sɛɛkɛɛ - March
Wal wali - April
Yanthoŋ/yanthome - May
Womandi/tutala - June
Paaya - July
Wuyɔ wuyɔ - August
Gbɔthikɔ - September
Fosoŋ/kufosoŋ - October
Tharekethe/miŋ pɔyna - November
Thananthiya – December

Names as Pleas to God.
Kaanu – God (A boy's name)
Ba Kaanu – In the name of God (Aboy's name)

CHAPTER 7

Semantics

Section 7

7.1 Synonymy in Limba

Synonymy in Limba is derived mainly from dialectal variation in the language. Among the thirteen or more Sierra Leonean languages, Limba has got the highest number of dialectal variations. The Limba language is said to have 14 dialects. Among these are Biriwa, Safroko, Sella, Tonko, Wara Wara, Sonko, Kamukeh, Kelen, Mank ɔ, Kalanthuba, Simiria,Kamukeh. Historically the Limba are said to have been the only aborigines of Sierra Leone who had occupied the Wara Wara Mountains in Koinadugu District. Over the centuries, they had migrated southwards and northwest occupying lands that are today called Bombali , Port Loko, Kambia and Tonkolili Districts. Those that remained in the Wara Wara Mountain range in Koinadugu District are known as the Wara Wara, Sonko and Kamukeh. Those that settled in Bombali District are the Biriwa, Safroko and Sella. Kelen – a mixture of Biriwa and Sonko; and Bimanko - a mixture of Biriwa and Safroko, also live in Bombali District – in the east and south of the District. The Sella Limba are the group that occupied the north of Bombali, while the Tonko are those that crossed over the Little Scarcies in Kambia District and TMS Chiefdoms in Port Loko District or North-West Region. Those that live in the north of Tonkolili are referred to as the Simiria and Kalanthuba. Both dialects have got a heavy mixture of Safroko and slightly Koranko.

In a sense, the Limba ethnic group can be said to have five (5) major dialects, judging by the number of speakers. The 5 main dialects are:
Biriwa, Safroko, Wara Wara, Sella and Tonko. The fact that all the major dialects hail from the same region, the Wara Wara Mountains, accounts for a common understanding of the language by all speakers of the dialects. Except for the few vocabulary

71

borrowed from other ethnic groups like Themne, Soso, Yalunka etc, meaning is not distorted. In fact intonation generally marks the differences in the dialects.

7.2 Synonymy Among Dialects

Biriwa	Safroko	Wara Wara	Sella	Tonko	Meaning
Nsɛɛ	Nsɛɛ	hɛrɛbahure	hɛribahure	hɛribahure	Good morning
nsɛ bena	nsɛ bena	manbena	heribahure bena	heribahure bena	Good morning(to 2+more
Nwali	Nwali	hɛrɛbayiɲe	heribayiɲe	heribayiɲe	Good afternoon/evening
Sankaa	Sankaa	Belɛnde	Masankaa	Masankaa	Good night
nwali	Nwali	nwali	mamo	mamo	Good day at work/thank you
huyaa	Feefa	huyahaa	Yaha	yaha	Head
hulɔ nkɔ	hulɔ nkɔ	huyɔ nkɔ	yɔ nkɔ	yɔ nkɔ	hand
huthori	Huthori	huthopoy	huthopoy	huthopoy	toe
hutala	Hutala	hutaa	taa	taa	Palm tree
kupinthaŋ	Kupinthaŋ	ɲponki	kuthaanka	kuthaanka	Cassava
budɔmbɔ	budɔmbɔ	buponki	buthaanka	buthaanka	Cassava leaves
mpɛɛthɛ	Mpɛɛthɛ	mpɛɛthɛ	nthathɛŋ	nthathɛŋ	Potato
bupɛɛthɛ	Bupɛɛthɛ	bupɛɛthɛ	buthaatha	buthaatha	potato leaves

73

Biriwa	Safroko	Wara Wara	Sella	Tonko	Meaning
Thiiya	Thiiya	thɔɔya	nɔndi	nɔndi	True/truth
bambiŋ	Bambiŋ	ɲasɔkɛ	Fothi	fothi	lies
adɔɔyi	adɔɔyi	adɔɔyi	asɛthuwɔ	asɛthuwɔ	miscarry
Apiriɲ	adɔkɔ	Apiriɲ	adɔkɔ	adɔkɔ	Get lost
mawɔdɔyɲ	mawɔdɔyɲ	mawɔdɔyɲ	Siraboli	siraboli	Malaria
humpoo/bɔnsɔŋ	humpoo/bɔnsɔŋ	Kabila	Kabilɛ	kabilɛ	Extended family
husomba	hukɔtɔ	husomba	kɔtɔ	kɔtɔ	Pot
hunimpire	hunimpire	hukaayoɲ	huyimbire	huyimbire	An orange
Kɔpiri	Kɔpiri	Kɔpiri	kɔbiri	kɔbiri	Money
hudɛkɛ	hudɛkɛ	hudɛkɛ	Kutoŋ	kutoŋ	Riceflour (bread)
mɛmilɛ	mɛmilɛ	Sɛnkɛ	sɛnkɛlɛ	sɛnkɛlɛ	Mirror
sɛnkɛlɛ	sɛnkɛlɛ	Sɛnkɛ	sɛnkɛ	sɛnkɛ	Month/moon
Sansaŋ	sansaŋ	hukandaŋ	Kunku	kunku	Fence
hubulɔ	hubulɔ	Hubiyo	Biyo	biyo	A door
kɔmɔnɛ	kɔmɔnɛ	kɔmɔnɛ/ lahɔy	Lahɔy/ kɔmɛnɛ	lahɔy	Son-in-law
Marɛŋ	masiini	Masii	Wasi	wasi	Blood
mayɛlɛŋ	mayɛlɛŋ	mayɛni	Mayɔini	mayɔini	Phlem
kusakande	kusakande	Thasakande	Thapɛthande	thapɛthande	Junction

bapɛthi	bapɛthi	Kupɛthi	Kupɛthi	kupɛthi	Cover of pot/dish
Kiro	kiro/bathaki	saraani	Bathaki	saraani	Dialogue/discussion
fɔɔlɛ	fɔɔlɛ	hukotho	Kotho	Kotho/hoyɛ	stomach
bafɔɔlɛ	bafɔɔlɛ	bahɔɔyɛ	bahɔɔyɛ	bahɔɔyɛ	Pregnant woman
kayba	kayba	Keba	wathe	wathe	Male/male age mate
kɔthɔɔ	kɔthɔɔ	kɔthɔɔ/thethiya	Thaara	thaara	Elder brother/sister
nthonaŋ	nthonaŋ	Nthɔnaŋ	mbomaŋ	mbomaŋ	Illness
Abɔti	abɔti	Akasi	Akasi	akasi	To vomit
asalaŋ	asalaŋ	Asaasi	Asaasi	asaasi	Pour wine
kuthamba	kuthamba	Korokoro	Kukoro-koro	Kukoro-koro	Broad bean
thaanki	thaanki	thaanki	thehiya	thehiya	Maize/corn
lɔɔmbaa	kugbodoŋ	serekethe	thaanki	thaanki	Sorghum
hugbɔ ntoŋ	hugbɔ ntoŋ	husɔ lɛ	Hulontho	Hulontho	Okra
thehiya	thehiya	kuthehiya	serekathe	serekathe	Pearl millet
kupahu	kupahu	kugbɔmbɔ	Yankira	Yankira	Trousers
sandɛŋ	sandɛŋ	karagba	Bokari	Bokari	Head tie
Hugbanthaŋ	hugbanthaŋ	Hubɔpi/mukanayla	hubɔpi	hubɔpi	Earring

75

kuthurɔkɔ	kuthurɔkɔ	Yakali	Yakaliŋ	yakaliŋ	A play
Bure	Bure	Bure	Bure	bure	Boys' initiation dance
kupɔsi	Kubo/kupɔsi	Kubo	Kubo	kubo	Swamp
Kampa	gbolo	kugbele	Gbolo	gbolo	A portion (on farm)
Husela	husela	Husiya	kuthagba	kuthagba	A portion (on farm)
Kubiri-biri	kuloloki	Kubiri-biri	hubunthu	hubumthu	The whole of
Bisiya	bisiya	Bisiya	Binɔndi	binɔndi	Some people
atɛnkɛlɛɳ	atɛnkɛlɛɳ	atɛnkɛlɛɳ	Aduteke	aduteke	To return (sth/sbd)
adokoli	adokoli	Apoothi	Apoothi	apoothi	To be dirty
athɛrɛɳ	Athakaɳ	asɛɛsi	Asɛɛsi	asɛɛsi	To start
Adɛɳ	adɛɳ	ayenti	ayenti	ayenti	To marry
Handa	fanda	Handa	fanda	fanda	(your) father
haŋ	Faŋ	haŋ	Faŋ	faŋ	Father's side
handaŋ	fandaŋ	handanmu	Fandaŋ	fandaŋ	My father
huseŋ	hupɛtiyɛ	Thaseɳ	Seŋ	seŋ	Locust seed(seasoner)

76

mɛnthɛ	mɛnthɛ	mayɛnthɛ	mayɛnthɛ	mayɛnthɛ	Benni seed
Suku	suku	Suku	Kutɔnɔ	kutɔnɔ	Seed (reserved for planting)
Huneli	hunili	waadɛ	kuwaadɛ	kuwaadɛ	umbrella
Huyesi	hugbɔdɔ	huyensi	gbɔdɔ	gbɔdɔ	chair
Nsɛnɛ	Nsɛnɛ	Nsɛnɛ	thɔrɔ kande haŋ	thɔrɔ kande haŋ	welcome
atharɔkɔ	atharɔkɔ	apɛnkande	Akande	akande	To walk about
Funuŋ	Funuŋ	Hunuŋ	Hukele	Hukele	Sense/wisdom
Akele	Akele	Thaya tha ka-nayena	Thaya tha kele	Thaya tha kele	See evil spirit/withces
Sitha	Sitha	Yumba	Lumba	Lumba	Wait
Huporika	Huporika	Huporika	Huso	Huso	Madness/insanity
hutɔli	Kuhinti	Soha	Kuhinti	Kuhinti	Bed
kɔpiti	hopiri	kɔhiri	kɔhiri	kɔbiri	Money
Danthɛkɛ	Danthɛkɛ	Danthɛkɛ	Kunaŋ	kunaŋ	Report/account
Akikuluha	Akikuluha	apoŋkuyiha	Apoŋkuyuha	Apoŋkuyuha	To listen
kɔntɔkɔ	daminɔkɔ	kɔntɔkɔ	Danɔkɔ	danɔkɔ	Keep quiet/stop crying
Nfoye	Nfoye	nthɔrɔ/hɛrɛma	Nfe	Nfe	Sorry/my

77

					sympathies
masɔnkɔ	masɔnkɔ	sɔnkɔ	Poro	Poro	Noise/Very noisy
yɔnkaŋ	magbatiŋ	Lanɛ	Sɛkɛlɛ	sɛkɛlɛ	A joke
Limba	Limba	Yimba	Yimba	Yimba	Limba/a person
Thaniya	Thaniya	Thanuwa	Thanuwa	Thanuwa	Learn
Mathani	Mathani	Mathani	Mathani	Mathani	Learning
Asɛthiyɔ	Asɛthiyɔ	athɔŋ thɔrɔ	athɔŋ thɔrɔ	athɔŋ thɔrɔ	To suffer/struggle
Bamuyma	Bamuyma	Bamumaŋ	bahuyuŋ	bahuyuŋ	Birth attendant
Kusuŋ	husambori	Husambori	husambori	husambori	Bondo drum
Ngbeŋ	Ngbeŋ	Ngbeŋ	Nkele	nkele	Bangle
Kudole	Kudole	hudeleŋ	hugbolaŋ	hugbolaŋ	Bald head/shaven head
Hugbolaŋ	Hugbolaŋ	nabɔy	Hudole	hudole	Testicle
Malo/ Maloholima	Mabɔnɛ	Mabɔnɛ	Mabɔnɛ	Mabɔnɛ	Joy/happiness
Kaba	kaba	Kuthu	kaba	kaba	Pride
athikipi	athikipi	athikipi	atikiti	atikiti	To change/exchange
Athari	athari	Athari	Akiti	akiti	To run
Pataŋ	pataŋ	thankaŋ	Thankaŋ	thankaŋ	Has/have finished

78

Note: The Sella/Tonko dialect tends to drop the noun class prefix (hu) of many nouns. The two dialects also use the sound *y* where the other dialects use *l*, and *w,* where the others use *y*. Where the other dialects use the vowel *i*, the Tonko/Sela use *u.*

7.2.1 - Limba and Themne Words with same meaning

It is interesting to note that there are a few words in Limba that are pronounced the same, a few with distortion though, and have the same meaning as in Themne. It is difficult to say which ethnic group borrowed from which. Of course a few words found in Safroko and Tonko are borrowed from Themne because the Themne are their close neighbours and they inter-marry.

Limba	Themne	Meaning
Kufinti	Kəfint	bed
Yaari	ɛyar	cat
Mpende	ɛpende	millet
Pinkaari	ɛpinkar	gun
Kuyankira	ɛyankra	trousers
Kugbɛngbɛ	Kəgbɛngbɛ	pepper
Hupɔɔthi	Anpɔthi	cup
Ba digba	U digba	Digba
Rikɔ	Rukɔ	Rukoh
Bura	Bura	Bura
Yenɔ	Yenɔ	Yeanoh
Sinkabondo	Sinkabondo	Asst. Digba
Husambori	Esambori	Bondo drum
Sema	Sema	Old member(bondo)
Paaya	Paaya	July
Gbɔthikɔ	Gbɔthkɔ	August
Tolon̪	Tolon̪	straight
Kubɔri	Kəbɔr	The family
Mɛnthɛ/mayɛnthɛ	Mayɛnthɛ	beniseed
Panɛmo	Panɛmo	Greeting at second meeting - same day
Maseri/baseri	Məseri	A witness
Yagba	Yagba	Hurry/urgent matter
Kɔmɔnɛ	Komanɛ	Male in-law
Mɛmilɛ	Mɛmnɛ	mirror
Kusaala	Kətala	Small hoe

Kasi	Kasi	A fine
Gberekethe	Gberkethe	Very clear
Malankɔ	Məlankɔ	Kernel nut oil
Lɛmp	Lɛmp	Fast/quick
Kuthɛgbɛ	Kəthɛgbɛ	Slowly
Mabɔnɛ	Məbɔnɛ	Happiness
sɔbɛɛ	sɔbɛɛ	Hard work/steadfastness
Yiki	Yiki	Respect
yikthɛkɛ	yikthɛkɛ	disgrace
nthɔkɔma	nthɔɔma	Name sake
thaara	thaara	Elder sister
kɔthɔɔ/thaara (Tonko)	kɔthɔɔ	Elder brother
masɔnkɔ	mēsɔnkɔ	noise

CHAPTER 8

Numerals in Limba

Section 8

Makɔndi - the count/counting system
Makɔndi maŋ - the counting system
Kukɔndi - a census
Ba kɔnda - to count
Bakɔndi - an enumerator/one who counts
<u>Ordinary count with no object in mind or at hand</u>
Hanthe - one
Kale - two
Kataati - three
Kanaŋ - four
Kasɔɔhi - five
Kasɔnhanthe - six
Kasɔnkale - seven
Kasɔnkatati - eight
Kasɔnkanaŋ - nine
Kɔɔhi - ten

In counting, with object in mind, or at hand, the Noun Class prefix of the object is prefixed to **nthe** – for the singular noun, and its corresponding plural prefix is used from 2 upwards.
Wunthe (1), mule (2), mutaati (3), munaŋ (4), musɔhi (5), musɔmunthe (6), musɔmule (7), musɔmutati (8), musɔmunaŋ (9), kɔɔhi (10)-
The same pattern is used for counting from 11 upwards
Kɔɔhi iŋ wunthe- kɔɔhi iŋ hanthe - 11
Kɔɔhi iŋ bile/kɔɔhi iŋ kaaye - 12.

It is interesting to note that the counting system in Limba is **<u>Base Five</u>**. That is, the numbers start from zero to five (0 – 5). Any number after 5 is like one added to five, two added to five, three added to five, four added to five, etc. In other words counting from 6 to 9 is like calling five first and adding 1- 4 respectively.The next number is kɔɔhi (not five added to five). After ten, **iŋ/e** is put before the additional number.Eg kɔɔhi iŋ hanthe - 11 (literally ten and one) <u>Kɔɔhi e hanthe</u> - in Tonko & Sella

Kɔɔhi iŋ kale / kɔɔhi e kaaye - 12 - twelve (ten and two)

Kɔɔhi iŋ katati - 13

Kɔɔ hi iŋ kanaŋ - 14

Kɔɔhi iŋ kasɔɔhi - 15

Kɔɔhi iŋ kasɔnhanthe -16

Kɔɔhi iŋ kasɔnkale -17

Kɔɔhi iŋ kasɔnkatati - 18

Kɔɔhi iŋ kasɔnkanaŋ - 19

Kɔɔhi kale/ kɔnthɔ kaye - 20

(The Tonko and Sella Limba say **kɔnthɔ** hanthe followed by 2,3,4 ---on to 9 – The Biriwa, and Safroko retain the **kɔɔhi**, adding 2 3 4, on to 9) **kɛmɛ**, meaning 100, cuts across all the dialects. Again like **kɔɔhi/kɔnthɔ** – numbers above one hundred have 2, 3 4 and so on added. The Biriwa and Safroko use the usual count with regard to an object to add to **kɛmɛ**; the Tonko and Sela use the count with no object in mind.

Biriwa/Safroko	**Sela/Tonko**
Kɔhi kale - 20	kɔnthɔ kaye - 20
K.ɔhi kataati - 30	kɔnthɔ kataati - 30
Kɔhi kanaŋ - 40	kɔnthɔ kanaŋ - 40
Kɔhi kasɔɔhi - 50	kɔnthɔ kasɔɔhi - 50
Kɔhi kasɔnhanthe - 60	kɔnthɔ kasɔnhanthe-60
Kɔhi kasɔnkale -70	kɔnthɔ kasɔnkaye - 70
Kɔhi kasɔnkataati - 80	kɔnthɔ kasɔnkataati -80
Kɔhi kasɔnkanaŋ - 90	kɔnthɔ kasɔnkanaŋ -90
Kɛmɛ (wunthe) - 100	kɛmɛ (hanthe) - 100

Counting in tens from 20 to 90 is like calling ten first and adding 2,3,4,5---9

Note that where the Safroko and Biriwa use the sound l, the Sela and Tonko use the y sound.

Like numbers above ten to 19, the same addition of ordinary numbers is made above 20, even above 100. Whereas the Biriwa and Safroko use **iŋ** before the additional number, the Sela and Tonko use **e, -** both meaning **and**.

Kɔhi kale iŋ hanthe - 21   kɔnthɔ kaye e hanthe - 21
Kɔhi katati iŋ hanthe- 31   kɔnthɔ katati e hanthe -31
Kɔhi kanaŋ iŋ hanthe -41   kɔnthɔ kanaŋ e hanthe - 41
Kɔhi kasɔɔhi iŋ hanthe-51   kɔnthɔ kasɔɔhi e hanthe-51
Kɔhi kasɔnhanthe iŋ hanthe-61   kɔnthɔ kasɔnhanthe e hanthe- 61
Kɔhi kasɔnkale iŋ hanthe -71   kɔnthɔ kasɔnkaye e hanthe - 71
Kɔhi kasɔnkatati iŋ hanthe -81   kɔnthɔ kasɔnkatati e hanthe - 81
Kɔhi kasɔnkanaŋ iŋ hanthe -91   kɔnthɔ kasɔnkanaŋ e hanthe - 91
Kɛmɛ (wunthe) - 100   kɛmɛ (hanthe)- 100
Kɛmɛ wunthe iŋ hanthe- 101   kɛmɛ hanthe e hanthe -101
Kɛmɛ wunthe iŋ kale - 102   kɛmɛ hanthe e kaye -102
Kɛmɛ wunthe iŋ kɔhi - 110   kɛmɛ hanthe e kɔhi -110
Kɛmɛ wunthe iŋ kɔhi kale - 120   kɛmɛ hanthe e   kɔnthɔ kaye - 120
Kɛmɛŋ bile iŋ hanthe - 201   kɛmɛ kaye e hanthe - 201
Kɛmɛŋ bisɔhi iŋ kɔhi kasɔhi - 550   kɛmɛ kasɔhi e kɔnthɔ kasɔhi - 550

Note that the Safroko and Biriwa add the plural **iŋ** suffix for 200 to 900. The Sela and Tonko do not affix a plural after 100. kɛmɛ stops at 900-999. a thousand is **wulu-**

wulu wunthe/wulu hanthe = 1000

Like kɔhi,kɔnthɔ, kɛmɛ, numbers after one thousand follow the same pattern, adding **iŋ** or **e**. It is good to note also that the prefix of the word/item counted should be taken into consideration while counting.

Wulu ka wulu - literally thousands upon thousands, meaning, one million and above. Is it safe to say **mili wunthe? / Mili hanthe** to stand for 1,000,000 (One million)?

8.1.1 - Makɔndi maŋ – the counting system

Masaani maŋ - mathematical signs

Adinti - to add - +

Agbinki/agbikinande - to reduce (take away some) - ‑

Afanande/afayni - to share (divide) ÷

Akɔminande (put in one place) - multiply **X**

Wuŋ kay/wuŋ tɛŋ/wuŋ fuŋande - equal to: =

Hubunthu - a whole (also means a pod of cola nuts)

Mathinkinande - fraction

kupɛpɛ - fraction

Gbaŋ - part of a whole

Gbaŋni - parts

8.1.2

Ba Malɔkɔ maŋ/lɔkɔ baŋ – about the time/date

Malɔkɔ maŋ - the time/date

Malɔkɔ - day/time

Mandɛŋ/mɛndɛŋ - days

Mathinki - second/ a wink of the eye

Sibiri - minute

Madɔnɔ - hour

Gbɛŋ - whole day

Kudu - whole night

Piri-piri - all night

Gbɛŋ kudu - an idiom meaning <u>daily bread.</u>

Wiki - week

Sɛnkɛlɛ/sɛnkɛ - month/moon

Hunina/filina/nina - year

Thanina/thaninɛŋ - years

Bayilɔkɔ - clock (literally the one that goes round and round)

CHAPTER 9

Section 1

Common Expressions, Synonyms and Euphemisms

Section 9

9.1 - Synonyms and Euphemisms

Thathinɔkɔ - bend down (also humble oneself)
Putɔ - bend down
Yupuŋa - squat
Thathina - put down
Dɛŋa - put down
Toŋa - drop
Yɛla - throw away
Gbantha - throw away
Thathintɔkɔ - recline (referring to an elder) also <u>stoop down</u>
Biye - wash somebody/bathe
Looka - wash sth/face, hand, foot
Looka - also ceremonial cleansing)
Gbɔka - scrub
Kaaniya/puthuwa/puthuya- wipe sth
Lɔsa - pull, draw
Lɔsina - draw a bit
Bɔla - draw/pull a heavy weight
Pɛtha - open
Kubuna - open (pull the cover of a pot/dish for example)
Nɔtha - push gently
Wɔkita - push hard
Thɔnɔkɔ - shift a bit
Thiya - put in
**Thiiya/nɔndi - truth, true
Fuŋuna - take out/bring out

Gbɔyna - take away from

Fuŋuta - bring out/take out/report on

Athimiŋ - to make sweet/make sbd.cheerful (literally). Also a vulgar word for sexual intercourse

Muthɔnkɔy - faeces (euphemistic)

Mutikiŋ - faeces (vulgar)

A kay ka feli - go to toilet (euphemistic). Literally - go to the bush)

Athaaki - to go to the toilet (vulgar)

Athaki bay/bɛy - to be in trouble/to offend

Athaaki mandi - to suffer (Literally – to excrete water)

Mayobɛɛni - hesitation

Hamɛ - doubt, fear for

Sikɛ - doubt

Asama samaŋ - to be in doubt of

Aŋele - to recognize

ayilɔ huya/fefa - abnormal behavior, mental problem

mapiraŋ /huso - insanity

madɔriyaŋ - reluctance in waking up from sleep in the morning

kathara ba /thɔkɔ ba – on behalf of

wuŋ thɔyande/thɔlande – it looks like…

asakati - to divert

asakitɔkɔ - take a sick person to a hide out/secluded place

wo bɔrɔ/ wo tewɔy - an old person/sth./animal

wo bɔrɔ bɔrɔ/wo tewɔy tewɔy - a very old person…

kɛbɔrɔ - a very old man

wu bɔrɔ/wu tewɔy - an old matter/sth./ long time ago

Athɔkɔti/amanbi - to stay long

Wuŋ thɔkɔti/wuŋ nambe - it has taken a long time

Wuŋ furukutu - it has taken some days/ a long time

9.1.1 -Proverbs and Riddles

thabɔrɔ - proverbs

athii banka buy ba somosi - Setting a house on fire to drive away mosquitoes - a senseless action

hugbogbo thare ta buy - Fire does no harm to the hugbogbo fruit. Therefore it does not run away from fire. Also somebody with long endurance.

87

alɔsi boro kamandi - To draw the alligator out of the water.= Diplomacy is needed to calm down an enraged person.

apithiŋ manaŋ ku paahu/kuyankira - Forcing a cow to put on a pair of trousers, i.e. a fruitless enterprise

atɔŋ kusɔlɔ ka peniŋ - Throwing a ripe palm nut fruit to red ants. They'll finish eating it in no time = selling a rare food/commodity to many hungry customers.

ngbentha serere kuthori serere - The bush fowl is never caught in a trap made from palm leaf string.i.e. No matter how a man thinks he is clever, other people are always cleverer

madɔŋɔ furuthethe – living together has fowl smells generally. There is need for tolerance.

mutikiŋ muka baahuyŋ – The dung/faeces of goats are always the same size. None is bigger than the other = persons of the same age group/contemporaries.

basema sa nine, bɔnkaa sa nine – the driller and the drilled; the trainer and the trainee

ndo iŋ bɔlɛ ka ŋathɛ - You have hair on your feet = you have dependants/followers. Therefore do not be rash in your decisions. Be accommodating.

bahɔtɔ kokire ta - A hen does not crow = women should not be voiceferous; forceful in character

akubuŋ kunanka - Opening the heel = problem of witchcraft arising from within the household/family.

Huthukeŋ mɛy kɛmɛ - talk of the devil and he is here

Budu kafunkulɛ - an easy access.

Ka ŋalee bara - where the meat comes from = It is always good to give to him a small share of the meat that a hunter offers you. Also, it is always good to give to him a small share of the palm wine that a palmwine tapper offers you.

Mandi ma sɛɛrɛ sa duthu - little drops of water makes a mighty ocean.

Atutu thɔɔyɔ wo ka huwɔɔ thɔ haŋ - adding a bigger portion to the smaller one. That is giving much more to someone that already has.

Theε wo koŋε maya na pothεy ŋa thay – the chicken that spills palmoil has its feet red. Meaning: the child that misbehaves deserves beating.

Kanu na biye ba budu – God bathes the leper (the one without fingers) = God provides for the downtrodden

Wundε yele kuthεy/kuthaki – S/he has thrown off the leg = he/she has died.

Manaŋ wo kɔtɔkɔy sa thiye magbuntu – the first cow to the river does not drink dirty water = early arrivals receive a bounty reward.

Agbuduŋ/adagbi pεlεthi ba thɔnkɔ/nεnɔ – to beat the chimpanzee for his ugliness = What God has made cannot be unmade.

athandɔkɔ - to be boastful

bathandɔkɔ - a boastful person / a braggart

apalani - to frighten

apalpalinɔkɔ - to threaten

athɔthɔn - to provoke someone

asumuye - to gang up to fight one person

athoona wu kahε - to be very sick

Mɔlɔn - price

Mɔlɔn ma kahε - high price, dear/expensive

Mɔlɔn ma yεkile - cheap price

Athinkinande - to break/to shorten a date for some work

akɔminande - to gather in one place

wounuyε - he/she is lazy (literally he she is rotten)

athoke fɔɔlε - a glutton/eats too much

kufiyo - eagerness/longing

9.1.2 - mpati biyaapa – Special riddles

kikiri kɔkɔrɔ - Two pregnant women can't carry each other on her back

sese keda seda - a needle cannot be stuck on a rock

gbaraŋ ŋate gbaraŋ thathe - pestle goes up, pestle goes down. i.e. two people pounding rice /other foods using a mortar and pestle.

9.1.3 - Tongue twister

Papa male, bathaha male, bathaha thaaki.
Bathaha male, papa male, bathaha thaaki.

Meaning: Papa jumped, deer jumped, deer defecated. Deer jumped, papa jumped, deer defecated.